FUNDRAISING WITHOUT BURNOUT

RADICALLY REIMAGINING PHILANTHROPY TO TRANSFORM YOUR IMPACT

RADHA FRIEDMAN

Difference Press

Washington, DC, USA

Copyright © Radha Friedman, 2023

All rights reserved. No part of this book may be reproduced in any form without permission in writing from the author. Reviewers may quote brief passages in reviews.

Published 2023

DISCLAIMER

No part of this publication may be reproduced or transmitted in any form or by any means, mechanical or electronic, including photocopying or recording, or by any information storage and retrieval system, or transmitted by email without permission in writing from the author.

Neither the author nor the publisher assumes any responsibility for errors, omissions, or contrary interpretations of the subject matter herein. Any perceived slight of any individual or organization is purely unintentional.

Brand and product names are trademarks or registered trademarks of their respective owners.

Cover design: Jennifer Stimson

Editing: Natasa Smirnov

Author's photo courtesy of: Andria Lindquist

CONTENTS

Preface	vii
1. The Fundraiser Revolution	1
2. How I Learned to Stop Worrying and Love Philanthropy	11
3. You Might Need to Detox Those "Best Practices"	33
4. Connect to Your History: How Fundraising Became Gendered	53
5. Connect to Your Self: Letting Go of Scarcity Mindset	69
6. Connect to Your Purpose	83
7. Connect to Community	93
8. Connect to Nourishment	109
9. Connect to Trust: Redefining Risk	121
10. Connect to A Vision of What's Possible: The Great Wealth Transfer to Women	135
11. How to Have Funds and Roses	149
Acknowledgments	165
Glossary of Terms	167
About the Author	171
Thank You for Reading	173
Notes	175

This book is dedicated to the unsung heroes of the social change nonprofit sector who work every day to create a better, safer, more equitable world.

Thanks to my wife Rosa, to my family, and to my chosen family, who urged me for years to please stop sending them emails about my crazy work experiences and instead write this book.

PREFACE

Of the many fundraising books out there, many are how-to guides for newly created nonprofits, offering a roadmap that treats fundraising as analogous to marketing and sales in the business sector where you follow a set of best practices in order to close the deal.

This is not that book.

There is a significant gap in the literature to address the truth about how the nonprofit sector functions as a result of its history, how that history has shaped the nonprofit workforce (predominantly white women who were otherwise not allowed to leave the home), and how women's historical exclusion from finance has defined the (often antiquated) best-practices we use today, in which fundraisers (mostly women) ask funders (mostly men) for "gifts."

This book is for anyone who believes in social change and wants to find the resources that can bring that change to life.

That includes anyone deeply committed to a cause that wants others to join them in partnership, including those charged with raising funds and resources for nonprofit organizations, foundations, universities, hospitals, and other causes.

While the majority of data in this book focuses on the experience of women in nonprofits – both because women comprise the majority of the nonprofit sector and because of the dearth of data about how people who are transgender, non-binary, gender-queer or gender non-conforming experience burnout – I hope this book makes you feel seen and included in a society that has historically been exclusionary.

This book is for you if you work in one of the 1.8 million organizations in the nonprofit sector in the U.S. or one of the 10 million nonprofits around the globe.

This book is for you if your primary role is to find the resources and partners to make social change happen, including fundraising and development staff, executive directors, or board members who support fundraisers as part of a culture of philanthropy. It is also for you if you are a donor organizer, philanthropic advisor, giving circle member, or volunteer.

I hope that this book will help you understand how we have arrived at this moment where our fundraising practices have led to so much exhaustion and burnout, and how we can change that by providing new approaches that will make attracting and working with funding partners easier, more effective, and more rewarding.

I hope that you will understand that the exhaustion you feel is not because you are not good enough, but because you are working within oppressive systems of patriarchy, white supremacy, and capitalism, where toxic productivity and perfectionism have made you believe that your worth is equal to the money you raise.

I hope that not only will you be able to raise more

money, but that you will be more aligned and integrated with your values, as will your partners and dream donors. I hope you will feel ease. And I hope that as you read the steps about how to prevent and heal from burnout, you will feel infinitely powerful, knowing that you are exactly the right person to do this work, and that you are offering a gift to everyone you interact with.

You may be thinking, "Oh no, suddenly this is sounding like it might be a lot of work, and I don't want to do any work because I am so overwhelmed already!" I want to assure you that, no matter what dimension of overwhelm or burnout you are experiencing, by reading this book you are giving yourself the opportunity to reclaim your energy and fulfillment. You have a powerful role to play in the ecosystem of social change, and this book is your permission slip to let go of the things that are holding you back from realizing your greatest potential for social change, even if those things are what you have been taught are "best practices" in the industry and you cannot imagine questioning them.

This book is about transforming and re-imagining philanthropy as a sacred opportunity to rebalance power. It is a guide to help you to detox fundraising practices that are leading to an epidemic of burnout among fundraisers, and to rebalance your life.

I share candidly in this book my own experiences working inside nonprofits, as well as my experiences as a grant-maker and philanthropic advisor. I have sat at many different tables, and in multiple chairs at the table, as someone asking for funding, as someone making the funding decisions, and as someone advising philanthropists on how to make their greatest impact.

I share this because I, myself, followed all the best practices, played by the rules, raised more money than I could have imagined, helped my nonprofit organization win prestigious awards from around the world, and instead of bringing me joy it was the worst I felt in my entire life and I burned out.

This book is my way of helping to prevent that from happening to anyone else, and to make my story visible so that others who may be suffering in silence know that they are not alone, and that there is another way of doing this work that doesn't deplete you.

This book is a love letter to everyone who works in nonprofits and social change work. I hope it can help us radically reimagine how we relate to one another to create a deeper sense of belonging. I believe in you, changemakers.

1

THE FUNDRAISER REVOLUTION

"Cows run away from the storm while the buffalo charges toward it and gets through it quicker. Whenever I'm confronted with a tough challenge, I do not prolong the torment. I become the buffalo."

— WILMA MANKILLER

I had one hour left to submit my grant proposal when the internet suddenly went out. I had just spent the last several days – and countless hours – painstakingly typing answers to the grant proposal into tiny boxes in an archaic website with miniscule word counts.

If you've ever seen the eighties' classic *Splash* where Darryl Hannah speaks her mermaid name and shatters all the glass in the room, that is what I imagine my blood curdling shriek sounded like to my neighbors.

For a brief moment, time stood still as I slowly processed what was happening, and everything that was at stake if we did not submit this proposal and seize our moment to receive this funding. Fighting back tears, I bolted out the door and jumped in my car to find the nearest coffee shop with Wi-Fi before the sand left the hourglass on the deadline.

I managed to make it to a coffee shop, bought the obligatory coffee to gain Wi-Fi access (probably my fortieth cup of the day), pressed "submit" on the grant proposal, and then ... ding! An error message. "You have got to be f*cking kidding me," I said in exasperation, resisting the urge to flip over the table like The Incredible Hulk, as I spent the remaining hour drenched in sweat and forcing myself to breathe deeply as I frantically raced to re-type each paragraph into each miniscule box on the grant application.

That story ultimately resulted in funding (and some gray hairs). However, it's a story that – when I share it with other fundraisers – elicits a knowing expression best captured by the meme where the building is on fire and the caption cheerily reads, "Everything is fine!"

In nonprofits, fundraising is constant stress.

We barely have time to laugh at these moments of panic before we are on to the next proposal, the next donor prospect, or the next fundraising event. Not one week later, I found myself standing by the stage of our annual fundraiser, drenched in sweat again with another crisis. I was on the phone with my keynote speaker, watching as hundreds of chairs were set up in the auditorium where she was about to take the stage in a few hours, as she told me that her flight was delayed due to a snowstorm and she wasn't sure she could make it.

My stomach dropped. I took some deep breaths and sprang into action with a Plan B, rallying a board member to step in as a last-minute understudy, re-assigning roles, and hand-writing new scripts as guests began arriving and taking their seats. About thirty minutes before curtain, the door swung open and my original keynote speaker arrived after all, having miraculously made it, and we were back to our original plan! (More hairs turned gray that night.)

Ah, fundraising. It's a cycle that is both exhilarating and exhausting. Fundraising is one of the most vital parts of a nonprofit's ability to create impact. Without resources and partners, organizations cannot achieve their ambitious visions to change the world. That means that the people who lead the fundraising efforts have an exalted and pivotal role in literally bringing dreams to life. Fundraisers are magicians, sages, and changemakers that help take an idea of what is possible (not just for the organization, but for communities and societies) and bring it to life.

To be a fundraiser also means walking between worlds. Fundraisers become shapeshifters that can walk between their modest nonprofit office with rickety, duct-taped, donated office chairs, to a donor's country club overlooking a lake.

Fundraisers have the opportunity to mingle with some of the wealthiest people in society, setting foot into powerful and often opulent rooms and homes that many of us can never enter otherwise. I remember some of my earliest meetings with donors and donor prospects, feeling a sense that I had "finally made it" because I was sitting with donors who deemed me worthy of their time, talking about an opportunity to work together to change the world. And at the same time, I felt so much discomfort with the power dynamics, the hypocrisy of talking about poverty with multi-million-dollar foundations while sitting in the most lavish spaces I had ever set foot in, stifling my unspoken questions about where all this wealth came from....

For years, I grappled with these contradictions, and they kept me up at night. I lay awake worrying about making our fundraising goals, worrying about what would happen with payroll, worrying that a board member would resign and take with them our best hopes at reaching new funders, and worrying I might accidentally speak my true mind to a powerful funder. When I was invited to speak to an ambassador at the World Bank, I thought back to my college-era protests against the World Bank's structural adjustment policies and worried that my values were clashing with my job responsibilities. Was it ethical to accept funding from them? Was it ethical for me to refuse and stand in the way of what the organization wanted?

Maybe this sounds familiar? You joined a nonprofit because you fell in love with its mission. You love the optimism of believing that a better world is possible and knowing that you are a part of the change. You are energized knowing that you offer an essential solution to a critical problem that is keeping us from having a healthier, more just and equitable world.

The challenge is, when you become a fundraiser, you also become responsible for making the organization's dreams come true. You are now responsible for whether it thrives or struggles. To succeed, you must successfully navigate a sector that is rife with inequity and ethical dilemmas, all the while being stigmatized for your role doing "charity."

This is especially true if you identify as a woman, because any role that becomes associated with "women's work" is paid less and considered less prestigious and important, and women constitute 70 percent of the workforce in the nonprofit sector. And it is even more true if you are a woman of color, a woman who identifies as LGBTQ+, a woman with a disability, or all of the above.

As a fundraiser, you are out on the frontlines. You are visible to all, whether you lead a successful event or you don't and then have to send that cringey email to everyone who attended letting them know your organization fell short of its fundraising goals. The stakes are high, because people come to associate you with the organization and mission you are working for, and you often must use your own social capital and call on people you know from other areas of your life, putting your reputation and friendships on the line.

You put your heart and soul into this work, and because of this, it is easy to feel a little beaten down and disheartened each time you hear a donor say, "It's a nice idea [to end homelessness / clean up the oceans / protect the rights of trans youth / ensure safe access to reproductive health] but we just don't think your idea will work," or, "Yes, we did fund racial equity in the past, but this year we've changed our funding priorities and will now be investing in sea otters," or, "Isn't your program just a drop in the bucket that won't really solve this huge societal problem? We're just not sure it's worth it."

Best-case scenario, you succeed and get the funding your organization needs to meet its mission. If you are lucky enough to get the credit for your work (and for most of my career, I did *not* get the credit for my work), your success now becomes the new baseline that you must measure up to and continue to exceed. That means next year, you must raise even *more* to be considered successful. Sure, you achieved an incredible feat and helped the organization reach a new milestone, but now that's just the new bar you set for yourself.

Worst-case scenario, you don't reach your goal to raise the needed funds. Now you must bear witness as the organization you love suffers without the resources it needs to help the community. You feel responsible knowing that the communities you are trying to help will suffer. You also know that your peers and fellow staff members in the nonprofit may lose their jobs, and you know that your own job is on the line as well. The dreams you planned as a team won't come true, and you're not sure your colleagues will still trust you. Everything is on your shoulders. It's a stressful and crushing weight.

It's no wonder that the average fundraiser leaves her job after only eighteen months.[1]

This is why so many fundraisers eventually burn out, some changing jobs, some taking a break, and some leaving the sector altogether. Ten years ago, the landmark study, *"UnderDeveloped: A National Study of Challenges Facing Nonprofit Fundraising,"* revealed that half of development directors (50 percent) anticipated leaving their jobs in two years or less.[2] The effects of the Great Resignation following COVID have not helped. Activist burnout and social movement scholars have suggested that burnout is among the most formidable barriers to the sustainability of our social movements.[3]

It's also why depression and mental health challenges have been on the rise in this sector, affecting many of us who felt called to step into this work as wounded healers because we, too, experienced trauma and don't want to see others suffer the same fate. It's why we experience secondary trauma as we constantly watch and hear from the communities that we serve getting beaten down by unjust systems, and must then repeat those traumatic stories again and again to potential donors as our currency to ask them for resources to help.

And it's exactly how I ended up writing this book.

The panic in losing my WI-FI just before submitting my grant proposal – or having a keynote speaker cancel just hours before our biggest fundraiser of the year – were not rare occurrences. Finding myself in those ulcer-inducing moments when the future of my organization's work was held in the balance just became my new normal. And no matter how carefully I planned, made spreadsheets, or designed sophisticated management systems, I felt as if I was completely dependent on the whims of our donors. It was an anxiety roller-coaster that I just accepted, without considering the long-term effects.

But it wasn't all ulcers and gray hairs. I also had moments of joy and exhilaration when a wealthy philanthropist we had never met called *us* – not the other way around! – and asked for a meeting completely out of the blue. We had no idea that he was planning to create a new award for nonprofit leadership and that we were about to be the inaugural recipients. And so, we found ourselves like deer in the headlights when the philanthropist asked, "What would you do if someone handed you a million dollars?" (It was like a fairytale and I was Alice in Funder-Land.)

Fundraising can make you feel completely crazy. That shapeshifting superpower can also make you question reality when you make a small salary and struggle to pay your bills in order to assure the donors that you are stewarding their resources well and not spending their funds on overhead costs, and then meet donors at lavish hotels or clubs you could never gain entry into yourself. Often, we are asking for funds from donors who made their fortunes from the exploitation of labor and resources, and now are granting us funds to address those very issues they caused.

All of this can feel demoralizing. Because on top of all of this, our work inside of these nonprofits is often belittled. Once, a colleague who worked in an oil corporation described my nonprofit work as, "Work you do when you can't get a *real* job, something to keep yourself busy while your husband does the *real* work." (Yes, they really said that. Out loud.) All the while, many of us who feel called to social justice work are painfully aware that this suffocation of patriarchy, white supremacy, and capitalism that we wade through each day is what led us to a place where we need nonprofits in the first place – because we must do the work our governments should have been doing all along.

To do this work is to contain multitudes and embrace contradictions and still keep showing up. I've never held any other role where I simultaneously felt so acutely aware that I had one foot in the future dreams of what could be possible, and the other foot stuck in an unjust world where resources for basic survival are owned and controlled by a few.

When you choose to do this work inside a nonprofit, it can feel like the weight of the world is on your shoulders.

I want you to know that *I see you*.

I honor you. I know your pain because I lived it, and I burned out. *Hard.*

And now that I stand on the other side – after giving myself what I affectionately call my "radical sabbatical" and changing the way I step into this work – I want to offer you a way to reimagine your role as a fundraiser. What if you saw your role as the most incredible job that is joyful and exciting and full of possibility? What if your work invigorated you and filled you with hope? What if, rather than chasing funders and convincing them to invest by repeating heartbreaking stories, you attracted funders who intrinsically understood what you were up against, said yes immediately, and couldn't wait to partner with you and invest in your vision? What if, throughout the day, you continuously felt a sense of gratitude and purpose? What if the social change you have been dreaming of came true and you were a crucial part of the story?

I wrote this book because, even after raising millions of dollars and helping nonprofits win the world's most prestigious awards for their work, I realized I did it all the hard way. I let the bastards grind me down. And if I had it to do it all over again, I would do it totally differently.

I believe there is another way. There is a way that can make you feel like a powerful warrior, refusing to play by unjust and inequitable rules, and writing a new future instead.

Once I realized these rules were never meant for me anyway, I shifted my mindset and reimagined myself as a bridge that connected incredible nonprofits organizations that often go unseen by funders, and the donors searching for the best way to use their resources to support a nonprofit just like yours. It changed everything.

This book is about playing big with your actual dreams for your organization and for your life, and leaving behind the toxic fundraising practices that have been draining you. It's about learning how to stand in your power and saying "no thanks" to donors who aren't aligned with your values. It's about recognizing and claiming your role in transforming philanthropy, particularly as we enter into the largest wealth transfer in history. Trillions of dollars are passing into women's hands over the next decade, and to harness that potential, it's important to understand how women do philanthropy differently.

It's about doing fundraising in a way that actually feels good and in alignment with your soul.

We all deserve to do this work with joy, not suffering. Unfortunately, so many fundraisers are suffering right now and leaving their jobs, causes, and movements, that we are nearing a crisis, with unfilled development positions across the country. (As I was writing this book, a colleague shared that she had 11 open fundraising roles in her organization.) The world needs you, and I want to help you free yourself from old mindsets that are standing between you and that joy.

I want more for you because you deserve it.

I want more for you because you are inspiring.

I want you to know that the world needs you.

I want you to know that you are powerful.

I want you to know that you have the ability to transform broken systems into more equitable ones.

I want you to know that although oppressive systems are designed to wear you down and keep the status quo in place, this work doesn't have to be defeating; it can be joyful and exhilarating.

I want you to know that you are supported in ways you can see and ways you cannot.

Are you ready to change the world?

2

HOW I LEARNED TO STOP WORRYING AND LOVE PHILANTHROPY

"Life is a balance of holding on and letting go."

— RUMI

Have you ever let yourself imagine what it would mean if all your fundraising dreams came true? I'm not asking what it would look like if you met your target for the fiscal year. I am asking if the issue that you are most passionate about truly had the resources, the inspiring champions, the brilliant ideas, and the sustainable partnerships it needed, *what would be possible?* What would that look like? Who would you want to be spending your time with as you did this work? Who would you invite to be part of this with you? What would it feel like in your body? What would it allow for? How would your organization be different? How would the field be different? How would the world be different? How would *you* be different?

So rarely do we give ourselves the space to dream. In

our hustle-culture where we glorify being busy, dreaming can feel counter to our goals.

Yet without dreams, what exactly are we striving for? How often do you take time to really envision a world without the oppressive systems that prompted you—through inspiration or through outrage—to get into this work? To look beyond band-aid solutions to a holistic, systems-level approach that recognizes we are a small part in a long march to dismantle harmful and inequitable systems, laws, policies, and cultural norms? To understand the role we play in breaking generational cycles of trauma and helping to seed a different future?

When we are deep in never-ending to-do lists, barely scraping by to ensure our nonprofit gets the resources it needs, this can feel like a ridiculous question. Who the hell has time to dream? As Gloria Steinem said, "Dreaming is a form of planning."

Many years ago, a "dream" happened to me. And I was wholly unprepared.

I had been working in nonprofits since I was old enough to get hired. I worked in phone-a-thons (yes, I was that annoying person who interrupted your dinner and probably part of the reason that your phone number is now on the "no-call" list), I worked in local arts organizations; I worked in holistic health and wellness organizations; I worked in meals-on-wheels organizations, I worked in human rights organizations, I worked in Jewish community organizations, I worked in Tibetan refugee organizations, I worked in civic education organizations; I worked in microcredit and women's financial empowerment organizations; I worked in land rights organizations; and I worked in rule of law and access to justice organizations. I have always been drawn to nonprofits, and I have tried at least thirty-one flavors in my journey to make the world a tiny bit better.

I was searching for the sweet spot where I could be most useful to the issues and communities I cared about, and where I felt my heart light up with that, "Hell yes, I love what I am doing!" feeling.

In every one of these nonprofits, our ability to change the world was contingent upon the resources we could attain. And although my role in these organizations ranged wildly from board member to program director to glorified intern (and many times, my title ended up being "Director of Special Projects" because nobody really knew how to describe the twenty different hats I was wearing), fundraising was always a part of it.

Fundraising is the constant in nonprofits.

Sometimes I was raising the funds directly, sometimes I was doing the research to find the funding opportunities, sometimes I was writing the grant proposals, sometimes I was creating the communications copy to explain our work persuasively and compellingly, sometimes I was working invisibly behind the scenes, and sometimes I was directly engaging with donors and prospective donors.

What was consistent was that as we planned our organizational goals, our strategies, and our programming, we did so with a keen awareness of the worst-case scenario – what to do if we didn't make our funding goals. We spent a significant amount of time discussing how to save on costs, what we could do without (bring your own pens), and how to be as lean as possible. More than once, I watched my leadership forgo their own salaries in order to keep other staff employed and our programs running.

Rarely, in all these organizations, did we ever allow ourselves to dream of what could be possible if we had all the funding we needed. With so much work to do, and so many people to serve, we didn't grant ourselves the time to sit in the powerful dream space and envision a completely different reality. In fact, the work culture often considered that dream-space to be frivolous, and sometimes even dangerous – a threat to our future funding if the donors disapproved of our ideas, a waste of time, and a selfish desire for "more." We worked, day in and day out, in a scarcity mindset, with the threat of ending our programs or closing our doors looming like an invisible presence in the room.

I remember living in my tiny one-room apartment with my partner and cat in a space that was so small that every time I boiled pasta or took a shower, the smoke alarm went off. I was surrounded by so much concrete in the city that I actually transplanted a weed into the tiny crack in the sidewalk by my front door – a weed! – just to experience the joy of watching something grow, and every night, car alarms from the parking lot just a few feet away from my pillow woke me up. You'd better believe I spent a lot of time dreaming of an apartment that was big enough that I didn't have to step over my cat litter box to leave my bedroom. I waited expectantly all year for a raise that might make that dream come true, only to be told that the staff wouldn't be getting a cost-of-living increase in our salaries because we hadn't raised enough. "Sure," I thought, "I can eat ramen noodles for another year," as I stepped over the litter box once again.

I fully recognize that everyone has trials and tribulations when they are first embarking on their career, and it's just a matter of paying your dues. The truth is, after years working in small nonprofits, I learned that it wasn't a rare occurrence or just a fluke to not receive a cost-of-living increase – it was the norm. Many years into my career, with two master's degrees under my belt, this was still happening inside nonprofits, but it didn't seem to be happening to friends and colleagues in the private sector.

The one year that I did receive a raise was because one of my colleagues had quit and I was asked to do both of our jobs while we spent months searching for her replacement. Another time, my CEO told the entire staff that although we wouldn't be receiving any bonuses or salary raises, we should be happy that we were receiving "psychic income" from our good work in the world. Imagine that statement being uttered in any other sector! I tried to keep a poker face, but all I could think was that my landlord probably wasn't keen on being paid "psychic rent." Still, I put aside my worries over how I would pay off my student loans, because I fervently believed in the work I was doing, and I knew it was changing lives.

Then one day, everything changed.

THE MYSTERY CALLER

I had recently started a new job as the associate director of development and communications for a nonprofit working to secure land rights for the poor. One day, we received a phone call from a newly created research institute at Claremont McKenna College who wanted to ask us some questions about our work. This didn't seem too unusual, since we ourselves were an institute that grew out of a university, and we were happy to share any information that might be useful to others. When the caller explained that they wanted to come to town and meet in person, I thought nothing of it. I assumed that it would just be researchers talking to researchers.

"How did it go?" I asked our founder and our CEO nonchalantly after they returned from the meeting. They looked like deer in the headlights.

"Well ...they asked us what we would do if someone gave us a million dollars," said our CEO.

We all stared at one another in silence as we stood in the hallway, blinking but not speaking.

We had never discussed that question in any of our staff meetings. At that time, a million dollars was nearly half of our operating budget for the entire year. It was a moonshot. We hadn't given ourselves the time and space to dream about how a million dollars could transform our work and our impact.

Like every other nonprofit I had worked with, we lived with a prevailing sense of scarcity. We prided ourselves on our ability to do more with less, to scrimp and save, to be frugal, and our metrics of success were often how much we were able to accomplish with so little funding. Need to fill three job roles with one staff member? We can do that. Need to keep overhead costs low? Of course our founder and our CEO can share a hotel room on that business trip. (Again.) And because of this, we were completely startled by the question and didn't have an immediate answer.

This was a turning point. It was the moment that I realized that miraculous things really *could* happen, and we needed to make the time to really think about the answer. What *would* we build if we had the resources we needed? What would that take? What would it look like? What would it allow for?

We took this very seriously, and we got to work very fast. We brought in a professional strategic planner to keep us focused and organized, and we carved out time over the following weeks and months to put our daily responsibilities aside and imagine together – everyone, including our interns. We talked about what we hoped for, what we always wanted to try, and what we thought would make the most seismic shifts in the world. We shared what we had learned from ideas that hadn't quite worked in the past, and what we would do differently given the chance. Collectively, we started shifting out of our scarcity mindset and these meetings became a place of possibility and abundance. The way we interacted with one another began to shift, too, and our office walls began to fill with new energy.

When we did respond to that mystery caller who reached out to us from the new research institute and set this transformation in motion, we now had an answer. We were filled with abundance and ideas. And what happened in response? *He gave us a quarter of a million dollars and then introduced us to his friends and networks.*

It turned out that this mystery caller was a man named Henry Kravis, founder of Kravis Koberg and Roberts & Co. (KKR), a successful investment company on Wall Street with hundreds of billions of dollars in assets under management. (His buyout of RJR Nabisco was portrayed in the early nineties film, *Barbarians at the Gate*.) Now, later in his life, Kravis had decided to create an institute that would celebrate leaders in the nonprofit sector, study what made them successful, and share their best practices with others. Our organization and our founder were the inaugural recipients of the Henry R. Kravis Prize in Nonprofit Leadership.

Literally out of thin air, this funder had appeared and granted us all our wishes like a magical genie. We had not arduously researched him, had not spent weeks developing a moves-management strategy, had not written and re-written precise talking points before meeting with him, etc. He had his own team doing research and due diligence and they called *us* out of the blue and forever changed our future.

For me, this was the first moment I had allowed myself

to dream about "What if…" and shift away from the familiar sense of scarcity to the unfamiliar trust in abundance. With so much possibility in the air, a new idea had sparked my belief that so much more was possible – an idea that literally brought us millions.

FROM MICRO IDEA TO MACRO SUCCESS

I had just moved across the country to take this job, driving more than 2,000 miles with a tiny U-Haul trailer hitched to the back of my car and a very unhappy cat in the backseat who flew into the air every time I hit a bump in the road. After working in a microcredit organization – which was then a radical idea to reach women who were considered poor and "un-bankable" by lending them small amounts of money to start businesses – I was incredibly excited to connect the dots between helping women access *funds* and helping women access the basic asset of *land*.

Land rights were not a particularly big topic in the nonprofit sector that people were talking about at the time, so taking this job and moving across the country certainly raised some eyebrows. But I was filled with youthful exuberance and starry-eyed excitement about the possibilities to link microcredit with women's land rights.

At the time, microcredit was just beginning to rise as a strategy to address global poverty. Everyone was talking about the promise of how small loans could unlock endless opportunities for the world's poorest people, particularly women. There was suddenly an influx of funding as research began to show that investing in the world's poorest women could actually be a powerful and sustainable strategy to boost economic growth by helping them create small businesses. This is because, according to the World Bank, over 1.7 billion people around the world (roughly 30 percent of adults) are "unbanked," the majority of whom are women, and this represented a huge untapped market for impact investors.

When I would tell people about my work in microcredit, they would often gasp to learn that women in some parts of the world could not access banks to open a bank account. I would remind them that for those of us in the United States, we often forget that it was not that long ago that women couldn't open bank accounts here either. (Thank you, Justice Ruth Bader Ginsburg!) That didn't change until my mother's generation in the 1960s. Until then, women had no choice but to rely on a man – their husbands or fathers – to gain access to a bank. So it's not a huge surprise that in many parts of the world, these gender norms about a woman's place being in the home are still enshrined in laws, and women cannot access banks or own property or otherwise control their own financial futures.

I was drawn to microcredit because it felt revolutionary. It flipped the system on its head and said, well, if we can't get women into banks, then we'll bring the banks to women. In small, rural villages in countries in South Asia and parts of South America, micro-lending organizations began organizing groups of women and offering small loans of $50 or $100 to buy the supplies needed to start a small home enterprise – a sewing machine to make and sell clothes, chickens to sell eggs in the market, a stovetop to set up a food stall, etc. Even though the majority of these women were considered too poor for a small business loan from a bank, because they had no collateral, microcredit organizations helped women to form small self-help groups where they could become guarantors for one another's loans. This sense of camaraderie and mutual accountability allowed everyone to be lifted up together, creating a social contract between women to help one another thrive and succeed. It also allowed an alternative to predatory money-lenders, which were the only alternative for a person or family in need of cash.

It didn't take long for microcredit to become a "macro" phenomenon, because once investors realized that women had a 90-percent repayment rate – far higher than anywhere in the world – suddenly everyone wanted in on micro-lending. When the most famous microcredit organization, the Grameen Bank, and its founder, Muhammad Yunus, won the Nobel Prize, microcredit suddenly became seen as the silver bullet for eradicating poverty and empowering women, with investors and philanthropists lined up to support micro-lending everywhere.

I saw a golden opportunity to leverage the excitement among funders who wanted to invest in microcredit by talking with those same funders about the power of investing in women's ability to own and inherit land. To me, it seemed obvious that the same fundamental issues that led to microcredit – inequitable laws that were created with the assumption that women didn't need access to financial systems to improve their families lives – were also the underlying problem when it came to land and property rights.

I believed that both microcredit and women's land rights could be stronger if they were linked as vital strategies to help women in poverty access the assets they needed to improve their lives and their communities. Despite microcredit's ability to help women gain access to financial systems, the women receiving the loans understood that since their husbands owned everything - their homes and all their property - they could simply take all the profits for themselves if they chose to, without consulting their wives. Without addressing the underlying systems and structures that reinforce gender inequality by keeping women out of the formal economy, interventions like microcredit may not work. And the best way I could see to create a stronger foundation for microcredit to rest upon was by also addressing women's land rights.

The potential for transformation through women's land rights seemed vast because the majority of people living in poverty in the world (78 percent) are in rural areas where land is everything. If you live in a rural area, land is your shelter, it is often connected to your livelihood, and it is also your place in the community. Without land, you are essentially invisible. You cannot access government services or vote. You do not have a full sense of belonging.

I could not wait to connect the dots between microcredit and women's land rights and to talk with funders about how investing in both of these strategies could be transformational. And so, when I started my new job, I was like a child on the day of a class trip to the amusement park, giddy at the prospect of riding roller coasters and eating cotton candy until I barfed.

I devoured everything I could find that referenced women's land rights in any way. I became a women's land rights "stan." I practically memorized one report in particular that focused on an experimental program showing that women's land rights reduced domestic violence in India, and on my first day, when I met the staff member who authored the report, I gushed like an infatuated teenager. She barely looked up from her desk and said, "I appreciate your enthusiasm, but we don't need a fundraiser, we need actual lawyers who can do this work," and then shut the door – in my face. (It wasn't the warmest welcome on a first day at work, but I've had worse.)

I brought up the idea of spotlighting women's land rights to pretty much every staff person, annoying everyone equally from the CEO to the receptionist at the front desk. "But you can see the potential in investing in women's land rights, right? Right?" There was, understandably, hesitation. This hadn't been funded in the past, and many saw it as a dead end and told me to forget it. Other staff before me had led some projects to study women's land rights and learned that funders were not particularly interested in funding it. Although they had valiantly pleaded their case, without funding, the organization's leadership had no choice but to move on to other projects that could get funding, and so many of the staff who had led the gender projects had come and gone.

I wasn't deterred, and brought up the idea to a board member at my first board of directors meeting. He took a long look at me and then responded by saying, "Radha, if we put a 'gender lens' on our work, then people will think of us as a women's organization and we will lose our credibility." I was speechless.

My uphill battle continued like this until our development director left, and I temporarily assumed the mantle as we searched for her replacement. (Sound familiar?) We ultimately hired a fundraising consultant to come onboard for a while as our acting development director, and she brought with her a burst of energy from someone used to delivering quick results for her clients. On her first day, she and I sat down together to get her up to speed and begin planning our strategy and tactics for the year. As we were plastering the wall with sticky notes, she asked me what one thing I would do that I thought would make the greatest difference for the organization's impact. I had never been asked that question, but I knew exactly what the answer was without missing a beat: We should focus on women's land rights, and invest in storytelling to explain why this was so transformational.

"I love this idea!" she chimed. I had a comrade.

We knew that persuading the board and leadership would need to be carefully-planned, and that the best way to convince them would be through funding partnerships. The objections had been due to a perception that nobody would fund this, so all we had to do was find the funding. (I say this as though finding funding for any underinvested field is easy!)

We decided to start with a small fundraising and friend-raising event, so that this wouldn't seem overwhelming and people could warm up to the idea. We invited a former staff member who had led much of the organization's research in the past to share her high-level findings. She was somewhat hesitant. "Are you sure about this?" she asked. "The last time I shared these findings with a funder, it didn't go over very well..." We did our best to assuage her and although we actually had no idea if this idea would work, we had copious amounts of enthusiasm and optimism.

We held a small, breakfast event and our goal was to have 50 people in attendance. We just needed to show that people really did care about this issue enough to wake up early and hear more about it, and to sell enough seats to cover our costs and perhaps raise some additional funds.

The event was sold out with standing room only.

Sure, it was only the first step, and sure, it was only a small event, but it was a very powerful and important step. We had done it!

This was the moment that our mindsets changed. What happened from there was like a wildfire.

With the confidence of a successful inaugural event under our belts, we decided to "go big or go home," and held an even bigger event to share the importance of women's land rights on International Women's Day, renting out the city's symphony house downtown. We secured the perfect keynote speaker – the head of the newly launched Nike Foundation - who linked the issue of women's land rights to the work the Nike Foundation was spearheading to invest in adolescent girls. This was an incredible stroke of luck, because once our name became linked to the Nike Foundation and their Girl Effect campaign, we were able to open doors that had previously been closed, including entry into the Clinton Global Initiative (CGI).

If you aren't familiar with CGI, this was a powerful and exclusive event created by President Clinton in 2005 to bring together world leaders, business executives, nonprofit leaders, and philanthropists to match resources with those doing good work on the ground. An invitation-only event with high levels of security, the ticket to get inside required every participant to make a Commitment to Action to solve a specific global challenge.

It was a tremendous opportunity to be in the room with Nobel Prize laureates, celebrities, and major philanthropists, and it was the push we needed to kickstart our work on women's land rights unlike anything we had done before. We began putting our dreams on paper and before we knew it, we had created a proposal (and a CGI Commitment) to create the world's first Global Center for Women's Land Rights.

Everything began to change rapidly. With the strong foundation of an ambitious strategic plan that we had created by dreaming together, with the networks we had garnered from winning the Kravis Prize, and with the newfound confidence from two successful events on women's land rights, we *believed* we could do this. And we did.

In a little over a year, we had received nearly $20

million in new grants from some of the world's largest foundations - the Bill & Melinda Gates Foundation, the Omidyar Network, the Nike Foundation, and the Ford Foundation - quadrupling our budget. We began to hire new staff like crazy, doubling our headquarters in the US, growing our team in China, and opening four new offices in different states in India.

If ever there was a time in my life where I felt like Scrooge McDuck swimming in a pool filled with golden coins, it was this moment.

Things happened so fast (too fast) that suddenly I wasn't sure I was in the same nonprofit organization anymore. We had been working so fast and furious to write our grant proposals and the dozens of attachments to go along with them that we hadn't fully built the infrastructure to absorb this much cash yet, nor did we have systems in place to rapidly grow our team so quickly. It felt as though all I did for a year was work on job descriptions, participate in interviews, and deliberate new hires. Our organization charts continued to change so quickly that it was hard to keep up with them, because we were finding that once we hired someone, the job description hadn't completely captured what we needed them to do. My role changed too, as we finally had enough resources for me to take off my multiple hats. My job was split into three full-time positions – a director of advocacy, a director of communications, and a director of fundraising (all of whom came to me within their first months of being hired and asked how the hell I did all this on my own), and we also created multiple new roles to lead the newly created center for women's land rights.

Our magnetic glow continued to attract more funding. Not long after we received those large grants, we won the prestigious Skoll Prize for Social Entrepreneurship, an award we had tried (unsuccessfully) to win before and which required an organization to wait two years before applying again. Once the snowball began rolling, it felt like we might never have to worry about funding again.

Everything felt abundant. The way we saw ourselves began to change. The way others saw us began to change. We had all the funding support we needed and we were on top of the world.

But with all the new funding, our internal culture also began to change. We had been a small organization of twenty-some people working very closely together. For the good of the whole, we all wore multiple hats when needed, and we all pitched in. Our organizational structure felt very flat and we had a very family-like dynamic. The CEO and his wife invited me over to their home for meals, and I went out to happy hours with my fellow colleagues after work. I reported directly to the CEO, and when I needed to talk with him, I simply knocked on his door and asked, "Do you have a minute?"

Within a year of receiving this influx of funding, everything had changed. Now if I needed to chat with my boss about a donor, my question was intercepted by his new executive assistant, who literally stood in the doorway of his office to block me with arms-crossed and told me matter-of-factly, "You'll need to send a formal email requesting a meeting with the CEO. According to our newest organizational chart, you no longer qualify to send him direct emails, and I can already tell you from looking at his calendar that his next appointment won't be for at least several weeks."

Work stopped feeling exciting and started feeling exhausting. Clashes between "new staff" and "old staff" began to brew, new hires sought to put their own fingerprint on the programs to show their value, and suddenly the environment felt like a cut-throat political war zone. There were fights over budgets and who got what share of our new resources. Hierarchy sprang up overnight, closing doors that had always been open. I was no longer allowed to talk with our donors directly, and I was no longer invited to our board meetings, after meeting with them regularly over informal working committees where we split sandwiches for the last couple of years. I suddenly began learning about meetings I hadn't been invited to where decisions were made that had a direct bearing on my work.

Power moves were plotted, and good employees – both old and new – were pushed out.

I was one of the casualties.

Not long after helping the organization to raise more money than they had ever seen, I was told my position was no longer needed, given all the organizational changes.

Just like that. (I can't snap my fingers very well, but if I could, I would snap them right here.)

THE SHIT HITS THE FAN

I couldn't understand what had happened. I had done everything right. I had met all my job responsibilities, we had surpassed our goals, and still somehow it wasn't enough.

I had worked diligently, not just here, but my entire career. I had devoted years in unpaid internships around the world. I had volunteered everywhere from the United Nations to local food banks. I had spent years working late hours and always saying yes. I had completely dedicated myself to my work, knocking over personal boundaries left and right to put my work before my own needs. *Sleep? Who needs it. Lunch? A power bar counts, right?*

Another missed dinner with my partner? I'll make it up to them.

I had amassed considerable student loans by getting multiple master's degrees. *Sure, I can work a full-time job while also getting a double master's degree, why not?* And then I went on to do a post-graduate program.

I did everything I was told to do to succeed. I played by the rules and I was patient. I had been the good girl. And yet, instead of feeling accomplished, I felt duped. I felt depleted of all my hope and optimism. I felt as though once again, someone else was getting the credit. I felt completely drained of energy and devoid of any satisfaction in my work. I dreaded getting out of bed and going to work.

It wasn't just that my snow-globe had been shaken up – I felt as though my snow-globe had been smashed and drained. After raising the funds to make our dreams come true, winning these awards to help share our ideas with the world, launching an entire new center that was contributing to building the field for women's land rights , I should have been elated by this golden opportunity. And yet, I had never felt worse.

I had no gas left in my tank. I'm talking completely depleted of all energy, filled with imposter syndrome, convinced I was a complete failure and all my fundraising successes must have been a fluke, not sure if I should even be in the nonprofit sector at all, standing in my pajamas while sob-singing to Cat Stevens, *completely burned out.*

As I was beginning to pack up my office plants and sniffle my goodbyes, our new Chief Development Officer asked for a moment of my time and invited me into his office. "I know that I am new here, and watching what just happened, I wouldn't blame you if you wanted to walk out the door and never look back. But before you do that…I want to extend an offer to consider joining my team." I was completely puzzled.

The entire fundraising team was brand new, he explained, as were the program teams in all of our newly opened offices. With so much new growth from our fundraising success, these new teams didn't yet have relationships with the funders. The organization was experiencing growing pains and still finding its footing when it came to donor relationships.

Everyone seemed frustrated.

The local program teams were frustrated because they thought they were providing updates to the funders as requested and didn't understand why the donors were asking for more information. *We just sent a progress report, what more do these funders want?* The donors were frustrated because they had just made a sizeable investment in the organization and were not receiving the information they wanted to understand how, or if, the programs were working. *We don't understand what is happening and whether the programs are working or not. Should we continue investing? Should we stop investing? Should we consider scaling?* And the development staff was frustrated because they knew what was on the line if the funders pulled their investment. *If we lose these funders, we will lose momentum, need to cut staff, and it could damage our chances of future funding.*

What was missing was the connective tissue – someone who had the institutional memory, understood the big picture of what we were building, and could explain what was happening to our funders and contextualize it within the arc of our story. We also needed a translator who could be a wayfinder for both the donors and the staff, as we worked out the kinks in our communication. And we needed someone who could build the capacity of the new staff to set them and the entire organization up for success.

Although I was emotionally exhausted, I knew that this last mile was important. If we lost our funding now because the donors weren't getting what they needed, then everything I had worked so hard to build would fall apart and everyone would lose - especially the communities we were helping. It was more important than my ego.

I agreed to stay and help in this new role, as a way to close out my time with the organization intentionally. I spent the next year building that connective tissue alongside the donors, the program staff, and the development team. I listened deeply to what the donors were saying and asking, what our local program teams were saying and asking, and helping them to better understand one another. I was a translator, a bridge, and a team builder, working to get everyone on the same page.

I built reporting templates and example reports to serve as models in order to ease the burden on the local program teams, so that they could spend more time focusing on their work and less time creating reports for donors. When we submitted that first new report to our donors, it was a complete 180. They went from being unsure about their investment to telling us they were thrilled with our progress and asking if we would be willing to share the templates as a model exemplar for their other grantee partners to follow.

As I slowly began healing from the trauma of rocketing to the most successful and inspiring time of my career to plummeting to the most painful time of my career, I spent a lot of time thinking about how I would do things differently in the future. I thought about how I would advise other nonprofits going through these same growing pains. At the end of that year, I said goodbye to the organization that had been the love of my life and my greatest heartbreak for the last seven years, and I pivoted. I took on a new job and a new role as a grant-maker, rather than a fundraiser.

I was excited about this change in my career, because while I would still be working to advance social justice, it was an opportunity to sit on the other side of the fundraising table. Rather than constantly asking for funds, I would now be at the decision-making table as one of the people making the decisions about where to invest the funds. I was relieved to take a break from the responsibility of fundraising, and excited to use my fundraising knowledge in a new way to contribute to social change.

That grantmaking role turned out to be hugely influential in deepening my work as a connector between funders and nonprofits. It gave me the vantage point to understand the perspective of funders, and allowed me to help them understand what it is like inside a nonprofit. It helped me know how and when to push back on some of their demands from nonprofits, their biases when reading proposals, and reshape the relationships between funders and their grantee partners. It also helped me to work with nonprofits as someone who had been in their shoes, and who assured them that they could and should not be afraid to push back against donors, or even refuse money from a funder if it was not aligned with their values.

And, it led me to become a coach for nonprofit leaders (primarily EDs, CEOs, and fundraisers) to help them identify limiting beliefs, stand in their power, and build the boundaries and practices to keep themselves nourished so they don't burn out. Burnout prevention and healing are now core to the work I do as a coach and advisor, and I do it with the personal knowledge of what it feels like when your motor is running on empty. Now, I help leaders in our sector to keep their inner flames lit, recognize when harmful myths lead them toward toxic behaviors (such as perfectionism and toxic productivity), and help them hold the vision for a better, safer, more just world where they can make change without sacrificing themselves in the process.

Changemakers, I did it the hard way and I want to share what I learned so that you don't have to make the same mistakes. There is a better way.

3

YOU MIGHT NEED TO DETOX THOSE "BEST PRACTICES"

"If you are silent about your pain, they'll kill you and say you enjoyed it."

— ZORA NEALE HURSTON

It turned out that working as a grant-maker was a hugely eye-opening experience and not at all the "escape" that I had imagined.

In just a few short months, I gained a completely different perspective on how the philanthropic sector works. My new organization was a re-granting organization, meaning that we raised large grants from foundations, government grants, and corporate funders, and then redistributed them as seed grants for new pilot projects that were considered too small for most funders to bother with.

Sitting at the decision-making table, with all of our spreadsheets, matrixes, and weighting formulas for criteria, I quickly saw how people have very different perspectives about what they consider important, and how they think about risk. In my case, I was working to address issues of justice and was working with decision-makers who were trained in the law, but who did not have the lived experience of what those injustices felt like. This is not at all meant to discount the powerful work of lawyers or policymakers, whom I have worked with for most of my career. Rather, it's a reflection on how the people who often end up making the decisions have been taught and trained to think about risk in a specific way, and how that plays out when they make the financial decisions about who gets access to resources. For example, a proposal written by someone who was most like them - often another lawyer - was almost always favored over other projects.

Having a seat at the table for these grantmaking conversations helped me understand that what many funders thought of as risky investments was completely counter to what I believe about how change happens. It also helped me understand why so many projects that I thought were boring and status-quo were funded instead of some of the brilliant projects I thought were so unique because one of the decision makers thought the project's leader "reminded them of themselves."

Having a seat at the table for these grantmaking conversations helped me understand why women and girls receive less than 2 percent of all philanthropic funds, and why women and girls of color receive less than 1 percent. What I had interpreted as my own failure to secure funding for women and girls throughout my career was, in fact, a failure of our systems.

Through the next several years, as I slowly learned more about how the philanthropic sector functions, I began to see patterns and narratives. As the veils began to lift, I came to see that many of the things I had been taught were best practices throughout my nonprofit career were exactly the opposite, and were holding inequities firmly in place.

THE SYSTEM IS BROKEN, NOT YOU

The way we fund social change efforts is rooted in inequity, and it's costing us.

Much like teachers entrusted to shape the minds of our youth and future leaders, the way society invests in and supports the vital work of nonprofits is woefully out of whack with the way we treat and support millionaires, who may or may not be doing anything to help society.

The nonprofit sector is where the best of our humanity shines. It is where we recognize a need to protect and support marginalized people, communities, animals, and the planet, and we personally step up to help. Nonprofits are the safety net that catches those who fall through the cracks of our government systems. Nonprofits are also the watchdogs that hold up a flashlight when there is greed, harm, and lack of accountability in the private sector. Nonprofits are the vision-holders for a more just, equitable, and healthy world.

And yet, to work in a nonprofit dedicated to social change is to work in the most undervalued sector.

Perhaps because the name "non-profit" literally defines itself by what it is *not*, rather than what it *is*, we are often misunderstood. Many times, I have been ridiculed for the work I do, referred to as a "bleeding heart," a "charity case," or a "do-gooder," all intended to be pejorative for choosing to devote as much time as possible to tackling social and environmental injustice. (I've also been called a "white savior," but that one actually has validity.)

The fact is, if society were able to solve these persistent

challenges that nonprofits work on every day – alleviating poverty, addressing climate justice, racial justice, gender justice, disability justice, LGBTQIA+ justice, expanding access to health and education, etc. – we would have done it by now. So to mock those small and under-resourced organizations for not yet solving these global challenges – even as governments and businesses contribute to the problems, withhold funding to address the problems, or simply ignore the problems – is fundamentally whack.

The nonprofit sector is the third-largest employment sector of the United States, yet we are routinely treated as though our work is less important than business and government. Worse, we are often told by private funders - who are usually distanced from, and who lack the lived experience of these societal challenges - that *we* cannot be trusted with *their* funds.

This is completely backwards.

We are gaslighting the nonprofit sector, minimizing their role, and over-inflating the role of those with business acumen or simply inherited wealth, without interrogating this dynamic. We are ignoring the history of how we got here, and how it came to be that so much wealth was consolidated among the few to begin with. (Hint: Not by chance.) And, we are disempowering the very people who have historically made the greatest strides in every pivotal social progress movement from women's suffrage to civil rights: women, youth, and people of color working to advance social change. If we idolize these leaders and emblazon their images on our buttons and tote bags, why then do we push aside these leaders and opt instead for joe-the-white-business-executive when it comes to having a seat on the board of directors?

As I began healing from my fundraising "success," I came to the hard realization that not only were many of the best practices I was taught about nonprofits fundamentally flawed, but that they were actually designed to uphold the status quo – the very thing I thought I was fighting against.

This was a hard reality that shook me to my core. I had forged a career for myself based on values of equity and justice, believing that the nonprofit sector was the place to speak truth to power and right the wrongs of society. I assumed that all my colleagues who had also chosen this path had likely done so for similar reasons and were aligned with my values. I learned the hard way that I was overly idealistic, and that people had a range of motivations for being involved in this work that I couldn't always relate to. I learned that fighting for a more equitable world did not shield you from the trappings of living in said world, within the same oppressive systems and structures. And I saw that in fact, many of the best practices we are taught in the workplace are actually characteristics of white dominant culture, disguised as professionalism.

It was a wake up. I realized that somewhere along the way, even as I was fighting against harmful narratives and systems, somehow I had internalized these narratives and my brain had started to believe them. I hadn't even noticed it happening, but because I was surrounded by it, now I was filled with toxic thoughts and beliefs. I spent years disconnecting from these harmful narratives and beliefs, but the work of detoxing is constant because we swim in these narrative waters every day.

TOXIC MYTHS IN NONPROFITS

In order to free yourself from these toxic best practices, you first have to become aware of them and be able to recognize and name them. The longer you allow them to become absorbed into your subconscious, the more likely they are to take hold and begin to cause you anxiety, self-doubt, numbness, and eventually lead you to burnout. It's important to name and expose the myths that can often take the form of "best practices" and pervade nonprofits and our mindsets. That means, we need to recognize these best practices for what they are – myths, created in a time long ago and far away, rather than truths. Once you begin to see where and how they show up in your own work, you can not only recognize them and name them when you encounter them, but you can understand how they keep you feeling disconnected from who you really are. It is equally important to understand how these myths take root in our minds and bodies, because without understanding this, it will be hard to interrupt and change this.

There are three sets of myths that I have encountered most frequently in my work, and we will talk more about how they manifest as barriers in the coming chapters.

The first set of myths is around women and money. One of the best practices I was taught when I did my master in nonprofit management was to look for those with the deepest pockets first, because one fundraising ask was more efficient than twenty smaller asks. This is what leads well-meaning board members to say things like, *"Why don't you just ask Bill Gates for money?"* during a board meeting, as though you and Bill are best friends on social media and he doesn't have a thousand barriers to prevent nonprofit fundraisers just like you from contacting him. Unfortunately, the fundamental message in this myth is that it leads us straight to those who have historically held, and hoarded, wealth – white men and tells us to believe that those are the people who have, and who should have, all the wealth. It simultaneously implies that we should not be focusing on women, people who are LGBTQIA+, or people of color, because of an assumption that they don't hold wealth.

If you are a nonprofit fundraiser, the odds are high that you identify as a woman. It is a societal myth which is present everywhere, not only in nonprofits, that women do not have as much money, should not have as much money, and cannot be trusted with money. It is also a societal myth that women should not hold high ranking or high paying positions in our economies because of this—that women don't know what to do with money, or are "too emotional" to use it correctly. This actually starts very early by telling girls in school that they are not good at math. We see and hear constantly that women should just "be grateful" for what they are allowed to have, that women should be a good girl lest they risk being labeled a bitch, and should play by the rules - rules that definitely were not designed for women. We are told that hormones make women too irrational to be trusted with money or power. These myths show up in the way we fundraise, from the language we use, to whom we approach as donors, to the way we approach them. For example, there were many times over the years where I felt incredibly uncomfortable walking into the private clubs, lined with photos of white men going back a hundred years, to meet with a donor, and felt I must do this even when I didn't want to because I didn't have a choice and had to "play by the rules" in order to be accepted and advance in my career.

The second set of myths is around toxic productivity, and the erroneous link that is made between our worth and our productivity. That is, only when we have raised funds for our organizations to the management's satisfaction will we be able to gain acceptance and belonging. Otherwise, we are deemed inadequate, even when all the odds are stacked against us. This leads us to work well beyond what is healthy for us, and often beyond what we are compensated for in terms of hours. This behavior has been normalized, and being "too busy" has become glorified as the norm and even twisted into a proxy for being successful. It's not enough to work 40 hours, because if you were truly committed to your nonprofit's mission, you would work constantly until you dropped. This set of myths is the fast-track to burnout.

The third set of myths is around power, and the belief that those with money should therefore hold the power. This causes nonprofits to cede their power to donors, and prioritizes quantity over quality of funding. It is clearly a myth to believe that just because a person holds wealth, that they also hold the wisdom about how to solve deeply entrenched societal challenges such as poverty and injustice, and yet many nonprofits operate as though this were fact. This also leads to eschewing risk-taking, which is vital to innovation and equity, because it risks displeasing the donor. We will delve deeper into this myth in the chapter on risk, which is incredibly subjective but often defaults to the comfort levels of donors.

Of course these are not the only myths that operate unnamed inside the nonprofit sector. There are many other myths that show up, especially around paternalism and a sense of knowing better than the "helpless" constituents or beneficiaries that nonprofits serve. But for the purposes of this book, geared toward fundraisers in the nonprofit sector, I want to focus on these three that I encounter most often with almost every client I work with. These disempowering myths, often embedded into our best practices, are actually sabotaging our efforts to mobilize the resources we need to succeed in our world-changing missions, causing us to become frustrated, sick, and burned out.

They become embedded in our thoughts and in our mindsets, within our organizations, our movements, and they take root in our own minds and bodies. They become embedded in our work culture, in our strategic plans and our theories of change, in our employee reviews and decisions about who is a good fit in the organization, and they shape the way we think and feel about our work. They create a disconnect in which we begin to question ourselves, our knowledge and our intuition, and we begin to feel so disempowered about our ability to change things that we shut down and burn out.

So how do we change this vicious cycle? This first step is to notice and name these myths, and to recognize how pervasive they are and how they disconnect us from our power to connect with the right donors. We're going to walk through seven steps that help us do this and reconnect us to our power. But in order to do this, we first need to understand how our minds are wired so that we can rewire the thoughts and beliefs that lead us to burnout with different thoughts that are empowering and remind us of what could be possible.

SOME NERDY BRAIN STUFF

Why are we talking about brain science in a book about fundraising? Well, first of all, I think it's super interesting, so I am inviting you to nerd out with me! It's also important to understand how our minds work, how myths like these become absorbed, and to know that *we should not always believe what we think*. Our brains have evolved over time to protect us, but our brains do not tell us the difference between actual danger and perceived danger (e.g. a grizzly bear vs. a grant deadline), causing us to freak out, exhaust our adrenal system, and totally burn out. Here's how it happens.

The prefrontal cortex of the brain is in charge of executive functioning, including problem solving and managing social interactions. The ventral brain, in the back, is an entirely different part of the brain that stores emotions. The anterior cingulate cortex manages the conversation between these two parts of the brain, what we think and what we feel. Buried in the folds of the brain is our amygdala and hippocampus, which are our limbic system. The way that these parts all work together is that the amygdala relates our long-term memories to our emotions and stores that knowledge in the hippocampus. If you are worried that you are about to receive a pop-quiz on neuroscience, and you feel like you might be having that dream where you are back in middle school and you walk into the wrong class and are totally unprepared, don't worry. There will not be a quiz on this, and it's only relevant so that you understand this: if something significant happened to you, whether a beautiful epiphany or a traumatic event, your brain stores the memory - and the emotions that came with it - together as one file. So when something happens in the future, your brain recognizes it, pulls up the file, and reminds you of those same emotions you felt in the past. This might be a sweet and welcome memory, like when a donor unexpectedly wrote a check for twice the amount you asked them for, or it might be traumatic and terrifying memory, like when a lecherous donor did something inappropriate because they knew they could get away with it, and cause you to feel like you are in danger.

The way our brains have evolved to keep us alive and prevent us from getting eaten by a T-Rex is by storing information in this way to get us to react quickly. But reacting *quickly* is not the same as reacting rationally, slowly, intentionally, and in a fully embodied way that listens to both our minds and our bodies. So, while this may have been helpful for our cave-people ancestors, in our modern lives this means that our brains are often telling us stories on a loop like the mixtape that once got stuck in my car's tape deck and forced me to listen to the Footloose soundtrack on repeat for several months. And the stories we tell ourselves may not even be true! They are simply invented by part of our brains based on an emotion we once felt in one particular situation in the past.

That means that we may find ourselves feeling a certain way about a situation – assuming that disaster is about to happen and totally freaking out – even though it isn't actually a life-threatening T-Rex coming to chomp us into smithereens, but rather a need to fill three tables before our fundraiser event next week, or getting frustrated with that stupid PowerPoint that keeps freezing while we are creating a deck for a funder to show that we have definitely made progress and they should definitely continue investing in us.

When it comes to social justice and nonprofit work, many of us have experiences that are traumatic – sometimes mildly traumatic, and sometimes deeply traumatic. We now know that second-hand trauma can affect us as we listen to the communities we serve and then we must repeat those stories of pain and trauma over and over to prospective donors in order to "make the case" that we need funding to help. This is called "secondary traumatic stress," which is defined by the National Child Traumatic Stress Network as, "The emotional duress that results when an individual hears about the firsthand trauma experiences of another." Secondary traumatic stress is related to other similar concepts, like compassion fatigue, vicarious trauma and burnout.

We might be experiencing this as we recount stories to donors of unhoused people suffering from physical abuse while trying to survive on the streets, stories of refugees dying on boats as they attempt to get to safety, stories of dead animals washing up on the shores after a toxic oil spill, stories of children losing limbs when they stepped on an old landmine, etc.

Often the very way that we achieve our goals as fundraisers is by repeating these traumatic stories every day. We repeat these stories in our emails, in our donor appeal letters, in our events, in our materials on our website, in face to face meetings with our major donors, etc. It takes a toll.

Our brains are wired to help us avoid anything perceived as danger, but they cannot always distinguish between something happening to us and something happening to someone else, such as the communities we serve. That means that not only may we be taking in second-hand trauma every time we tell a donor about the vital need for their funds, but we may also experience second-hand trauma when our colleagues suffer while doing their work. Years ago, I had a colleague who got into a taxi while doing field work in Kenya and the driver hit a person on the road and quickly drove away without stopping to see if the person they hit was injured or killed. I was terrified every time I got into a car while traveling for work for several years. I also had a colleague who ate something that made them so sick they were hospitalized while traveling in Eurasia, and thought they might die in the hospital. I have had colleagues who narrowly escaped an attack on their lives when a gay bar was raided shortly after they visited it, colleagues who were forced to hide when a gunman entered their Jewish nonprofit office, and I will never forget meeting a colleague after work and hearing her tell me that three of her colleagues – a doctor, a program coordinator and an assistant program officer – were kidnapped and held for ransom in Pakistan, following another staff member being kidnapped and beheaded. Even though these events didn't happen to me personally, our brains process these stories as perceived danger that could happen to us, and it affects our sense of safety and anxiety.

Just as each of us are different people who experience trauma differently, it can manifest in different ways. It may show up as avoidance (putting off talking with that donor that you had a bad experience with before), negative thoughts and feelings (self-doubt, imposter syndrome, anxiety that you won't be able to convince donors to fund the work and may lose your job), numbness (feeling detached from your work, empty, or numbing yourself so that you don't feel things so strongly), depression, anxiety, trouble sleeping – the list goes on. In my case, the trauma often manifests as physical sickness, especially stomach upset and craving comfort foods. (Since I was raised as a vegetarian in a family that ate health foods, my comfort foods are pretty hilarious to other people, but I know I need to pay extra attention to my self-care when I find myself chowing down on multiple heads of broccoli in one sitting.)

Normally, emotions rise and then pass, but they last longer when we fuel them with stories, which keep these emotions swirling in a loop that turns the emotions into moods. If we continue to do this without awareness or interruption, we reinforce the narratives and create patterns of moods. What may have started out as a fleeting worry about meeting with a new donor now is attached to a story you are telling yourself.

The last time I had a conversation with a donor like this, they asked me a question that I didn't have a good answer for and the meeting didn't go well and we didn't get the funding we hoped for...This meeting will probably be the same. I'm going to fail. Maybe this isn't the right job for me? Maybe I should find a new career path altogether? I was so happy that summer I was sixteen years old working at the ice-cream stand, maybe I should give up on philanthropy and go back to making banana splits?

In other words, in times of stress, our prefrontal cortex takes over as a survival instinct, and it isn't always rational. We are operating on old narratives and telling ourselves stories that lead us to becoming stressed and burned out.

So how do we hack these brain loops and take our power back? We need to reconnect with both our brains and our bodies in a way that is intentional and interrupts the auto-pilot patterns. To reconnect, we need to become fully embodied – that is, listening to the wisdom of our bodies and not just our thoughts. What is happening in our bodies at the same time we are having these thoughts? Is our chest feeling constricted? Are we having trouble breathing? Are our shoulders locking into place close to our ears?

Through my work with nonprofit leaders and organizations around the world, I have come to see each of us as electricity conductors with individual wires in a circuit board that connects us to one another and circulates power. When a plug is loose, or is plugged into the wrong place, we don't function properly and we do not have the power we need. Much like in Ghostbusters where they warn, *"Don't cross the streams!"* we need to be mindful of where our wires have gotten crossed or where we may have become unplugged and reconnect to our power.

These are the ways to reconnect yourself to the circuit board that fuels you with passion, clarity, and purpose.

7 STEPS TO PREVENT AND HEAL FROM BURNOUT

Through this book, we will walk through the ways that toxic thoughts, myths, and practices can manifest in our work and make us feel disconnected, and how to detox them so that we can reconnect and recenter ourselves. This is a summary of the ways to reconnect to the circuit boards that allow power to flow freely through us, and to recharge if our wires have become disconnected or if our battery power is dwindling.

CONNECTING TO OUR HISTORY

To connect to our history is to understand how it is that we arrived here in this moment. To do this, we will explore the origins of our nonprofit sector to understand who made the rules that govern us today and in what context they were created. To understand where we are going, we must understand where we have been, and recognize that when we hear phrases in our workplaces such as, *"It's always been that way,"* that we hold the power to write a different narrative and a different future – one that is much more equitable.

CONNECT TO YOURSELF

To connect to ourselves requires the same honesty and compassion that we would give to a friend or loved one. This means understanding how our brains work, recognizing the power of our subconscious minds, knowing when our old mix-tapes or inner critics are running the show, and giving ourselves the same level of compassion we give to others when we see the warning signs of hustle culture and perfectionism leading us toward burnout. It also means understanding that our physical bodies carry wisdom just as our brains do, even though we often believe that our physical health and mental health are two separate things. By "trusting our gut" rather than ignoring our bodies in favor of our minds, we can integrate and reconnect to our deeper wisdom.

CONNECT TO YOUR PURPOSE

To connect to our sense of purpose is to give ourselves a compass and a flashlight to keep us from getting lost. When we are connected to our purpose, we can achieve things that seem impossible. But this means discerning the relationship between our true purpose and our current job description, or what our friends or parents think we should be doing with our lives. When these are disconnected, we are more likely to feel resentful, unfulfilled, or to shut down and burn out. Connecting to our purpose will keep us moving forward even when the work is difficult and feeling supported in a larger social-change ecosystem.

CONNECT TO YOUR COMMUNITY

To connect to our community while doing social change work is incredibly important, and incredibly powerful, because the philanthropic sector has created "us" and "them" silos, even when we are working to achieve the very same goals. There is often distance between fundraisers and the communities for whom we are raising money, distance from funders, and often distance from other nonprofits whom we see as competitors rather than partners in movement-building. To connect to community is to remember that we cannot do this work in isolation, and to remember it is not about us, but about the greater collective.

CONNECT TO WHAT NOURISHES YOU

To connect to what nourishes us is to prioritize rest as an act of revolution in hustle culture. When it comes to preventing, reversing, and recovering from burnout, it is critical to prioritize rest, which is the root of the word "restoration." Understanding the different kinds of rest and which form is needed is vital to ensuring you have the energy you need to do your world-changing work. It is also key to understanding that often the most productive thing you can do is to rest and recharge.

CONNECT TO TRUST

To do the work of fundraising for social change is to trust – in ourselves, in each other, and in a different future. Just as we must train our minds to recognize toxic myths, we must also train our trust muscle. There are countless new ideas, new leaders, and new kinds of partnerships that could radically accelerate our progress if we did not dismiss them from our strategic plans and theories of change for being too outlandish. Trust that resources for this work are abundant, even when you can't see them, and that new ideas and new leaders are out there searching for you as much as you are searching for them.

CONNECT TO A VISION OF WHAT'S POSSIBLE

To connect to a vision of what's possible is to fully plug in to the circuit board – connected to our history, to ourselves, to our purpose, to our community, to what nourishes us, and to trust – in order to fully stand in our power. When we are fully connected in this way, our success as fundraisers becomes a forgone conclusion and we can approach the work knowing that we cannot fail. We are often so focused on articulating the current problems that we forget to give ourselves the space to dream of the solutions. Just as you give yourself permission to rest, give yourself permission to dream of a different future. When that mystery donor calls and offers you a million dollars, know how that money could make the dream possible.

By walking through these seven steps, we can reset ourselves and reimagine the way we do fundraising as a sacred role. Fundraisers offer a powerful opportunity to do something greater than we could alone, to come together in community to create meaningful change in the world. These steps can help us heal from any messages that tell us otherwise, that make us feel small or disempowered, and instead feel rejuvenated, connected, and empowered to change the world.

Before we walk through these next chapters, it's important to note that while I wrote this book primarily for fundraisers – for development staff, executive directors, the communications staff that create the messaging about why this work matters, and others whose job description includes raising funds – I am also speaking to funders, because we are two sides of the same coin seeking to mobilize resources for social change. One of our greatest barriers to progress is our siloed approach to the work, and the walls that separate us.

While funders are always welcomed into nonprofit spaces, the opposite is not always true, leading us to be simultaneously having separate conversations in different rooms about the exact same subject, with completely different input, perspectives, and information. That, undoubtedly, is also leading us to come to very different conclusions. In truth, we are in this together, and we cannot do this work without one another. We are in relationship to one another, and this means that when I suggest that fundraisers should push back on some of the toxic practices, this will require you, too, to change. And change is not easy. (Perhaps the biggest understatement in the book.)

No matter how difficult change feels, we need to remember the vision we are holding for our communities and the importance of coming together to bring that vision to life. Because despite the discomfort, we (especially funders) are making these decisions based on a set of good choices. Our communities that we serve do not always have good options to choose from.

We cannot do this vital social change work without one another, and we will go farther together. Like the African proverb says, if you want to go fast, go alone, but if you want to go farther, go together.

4

CONNECT TO YOUR HISTORY: HOW FUNDRAISING BECAME GENDERED

"Women belong in all places where decisions are being made."

— JUSTICE RUTH BADER GINSBURG

If you are reading this book about fundraising without burnout, chances are that you are a white woman. The nonprofit sector rests on women's shoulders, and it always has.

There's a reason why so many women have gravitated to this work to help their communities and care for people in need, and there is a reason why the sector is predominantly white. Today, between 75-80 percent of nonprofits in the U.S. are comprised of white women. Why does that matter? It matters because nonprofit work has become heavily gendered, and with it, fundraising as a profession. It also means that many of the societal challenges that affect women differently because of different laws and social norms have become intertwined with nonprofit culture.

For example, the expectation to take on multiple roles

and wear multiple hats? That is something expected of working mothers, who shoulder the brunt of the responsibility for taking care of the children, all the household tasks, *and* all of their job responsibilities in their careers. It is also something we see in the nonprofit workplace when employees are expected to do multiple jobs because of the need to keep costs low and appear lean to funders. The result? A workplace culture in which the expectation is to take on the work of multiple people, being pulled in multiple directions, and made to feel inadequate if you cannot. As you might imagine, this is a predictor of burnout.

How did we get here? To understand why this work became gendered and how we got here, we need to reconnect with the history of how the philanthropic sector was created. Let us journey through time and harken ye back to the turn of the nineteenth century when our foremothers created this sector that we now work in today.

A QUICK HISTORY LESSON ON THE ORIGINS OF PHILANTHROPY

Most people attribute the origins of philanthropy in the U.S. to Andrew Carnegie, the famous railroad baron whose fortune today would surpass many modern-day billionaires including Bill Gates and Warren Buffett. (Philanthropy exists in a number of cultures around the world, of course, and has been such a vital part of culture that is hasn't needed to be codified into law in the way that it has in the U.S.) In 1901, Carnegie published *The Gospel of Wealth*[1], a series of essays that lays out the moral argument for the wealthy to give back and invest in social welfare of their communities.

While this sounds altruistic, if you consider the context

of what was happening at that time with the industrial revolution, you can argue that his reasons for penning this essay were perhaps motivated by a desire to disrupt the growing power of the labor movement, which was a threat to wealthy business owners and industrialists like himself. (There is a great podcast episode on *The Ethical Rainmaker* that talks about the racist roots of philanthropy and discusses Carnegie's role.) At that time, the U.S. government had not yet developed social welfare programs to provide for the well-being of its citizens. Instead, there were mutual aid networks that brought communities together to provide support for one another, with worker's rights and labor rights advocates making sure that people were safe, healthy, and cared for.

Around the time that Carnegie published this sentinel essay about philanthropy, labor unions were helping to build and strengthen these mutual aid networks. All this threatened the industrialists, because workers – backed by these labor unions – were requesting super annoying things like healthy working conditions, a limit to the workday (which was then twelve-hour days, seven days a week) and basic healthcare – all things we are still fighting for in this country today, by the way. There were labor riots and strikes, including the famous Haymarket riot in Chicago, and Carnegie's essay was perhaps an attempt to quell the growing unrest. It seemed to work, because just a few years after the essay was published, the first charitable foundation in the nation was established. And, fun fact, it was created by a woman!

Margaret Sage was a widow who suddenly inherited a $70 million fortune when her husband, a railroad baron, died. She decided to use her inheritance to help other women by creating the nation's first official foundation. Now, this was 1907, so at that time Margaret was probably not questioning her white privilege or examining how the wealth came from the exploitation of migrant laborers, primarily Chinese workers who were building the country's railroad at the same time the nation had enacted the Chinese Exclusion Act to prevent Asian Americans from owning land and thereby passing down generational wealth. Instead, Margaret Sage was doing what she thought was most virtuous by sharing her fortune with those less fortunate.

This scrumptious little slice of history is significant because this is still very much how people see philanthropy and nonprofit work today, over a century later: a *noblesse oblige* that is the purview of well-to-do white women. Charity is still thought of by many as a nice-to-have, but not a need-to-have, service to the community. This is important because it affects how philanthropic and charitable work is legitimized (or delegitimized), appreciated (or unappreciated), and compensated (or undercompensated) and how that affects how we see our value and our purpose.

Shortly after Margaret Sage created her foundation, the U.S. government passed the 1913 Revenue Act which created the 501(c)(3) tax-exempt status for organizations created to do social good. This began to transform the country's mutual care networks into 501(c)(3) nonprofit organizations, because people could receive a tax benefit for donating to charity. This also shaped the way we fund and support charities today, because instead of giving to your local mutual aid network, you most likely give to your local 501(c)(3) nonprofit and write off your donation when you do your taxes.

As the country began to create an income tax on the wealthy, the tax laws were written in such a way that wealthy individuals could put their taxed income into charitable foundations and fully control how and where it was spent, rather than giving it to the government. In essence, rather than the government delivering social welfare to its citizens, the taxable income stayed under the control of the wealthy.

This is also still largely how philanthropy works today, and it is a major critique of the philanthropic sector. It's easy to see how, because these tax codes were rooted in racism and sexism, over time, more and more wealth and power became consolidated into the hands of wealthy white men. And, at the same time, nonprofits became the realm of "women's work."

THE NONPROFIT GENDER GAP

How did this gender imbalance in nonprofits come to be the norm? Remember that at the turn of the century, women could not vote, work, own property, or open a bank account. Women were still largely confined to their homes and kept separate from public life. Charitable efforts, however, were the one exception – for white women, that is. They were permitted to do charitable work and sometimes even donate with their husband's permission to use his pocketbook.

In each of their racially segregated communities, women were the ones to mobilize and provide services like food and housing to people living in poverty, particularly widows and orphans. So long as their efforts were concentrated on charitable efforts, this kind of work was socially acceptable. Participating in any meaningful discussions about economic empowerment, social injustice, or political inclusion through policy change, however, was forbidden.

The birth of the 501(c)(3) sector created space for white women to exist outside their homes and access an alternative method of power over their lives and their communities. (Black, indigenous, and other women of color continued to do this same work through vibrant mutual aid networks throughout Black communities, Latinx communities, and Asian communities.) And when new labor laws in the 1960s allowed white women to formally enter the workforce and open their own bank accounts, tens of thousands of college-educated, stay-at-home mothers began starting nonprofit organizations by the thousands.

This journey back in time tells us why, today, women make up 75-80 percent of nonprofits and philanthropic organizations (white women are 70 percent)[2,3]

And yet, only 17 percent of nonprofits have a woman CEO.

Why is this so and why does it matter? In a word, sexism. That thing that tells women that we are worth less and therefore deserve less – less rights, less pay, and less power. It does a number on our sense of worth and our sense of power. It also underpins the kinds of trauma that we endure in the workplace that can lead us to burn out, either because we feel we need to prove ourselves or because we feel it is what is expected of us by society and we don't have a choice.

While there are more women in leadership positions in nonprofits now than there were a hundred years ago when the 501(c)(3) tax exemption status was created, it's still a hard climb. Once a nonprofit has a budget that exceeds a million dollars, women's representation as executive leaders or board members declines.[4] And, unsurprisingly, that climb is harder for women of color who are the least likely to hold leadership positions at nonprofits or foundations. This is true for executive director positions as well as fundraising positions.

Although women are well represented in fundraising roles throughout the nonprofit sector, once women reach the executive management level, that 80 percent figure flips. *While 80 percent of nonprofit staff are women, they hold only 20 percent of the senior fundraising roles.* 80 percent of senior fundraiser positions are held by men.

In some ways, this data shouldn't be surprising. We all know that the gender pay gap has been stubbornly slow to change across all our labor sectors. We often hear that for every dollar a man makes, women make only 77 cents. That is, of course, 77 cents for a white woman. According to this year's census data, for every dollar paid to a white man, Asian American, Native Hawaiian, and Pacific Islander women are paid 75 cents, Black women are paid 64 cents, Latina women are paid 54 cents, and Native American women are paid 51 cents.[5]

We also know that men predominantly control the business and government sectors, holding 93 percent of the CEO positions at S&P 500 companies, and more than 75 percent of political offices. Because of this, there is an important power imbalance to keep in mind that significantly affects the work of fundraisers: the money that funds the nonprofit sector comes largely from the profits of business (predominantly led by men) and government sectors (also predominantly led by men), and this has had a tremendous impact on how we fundraise – both who we target as donors and how we approach those appeals in ways that are marketed to men in business. (Return on investment! Metrics of impact!) It also explains why less than two percent of funding is allocated to nonprofit organizations that specifically focus on women and girls.

Understanding these gender gaps is important in understanding who created those best practices myths that shape our nonprofit workplaces today. Understanding how those myths were shaped helps us understand their consequences, not only for our career growth, but for our mental health and well-being. There are several problematic messages that often show up in my client's work, and they are deeply embedded in our collective subconscious. One is the underlying message that women cannot be trusted with money, and the other is that women should not complain about the inequities, but should instead be good girls and play by the rules if they want to succeed. Let's talk about how this plays out and why it is so significant to your fundraising success and in your nonprofits overall.

MYTHS ABOUT WOMEN, MONEY, AND POWER IN OUR WORKPLACES

The truth is, simply because nonprofit fundraising roles are predominantly held by women, we pay that role less.

It's an infuriating and universal truth that is present across industries and sectors. Because women's labor is so devalued, the average pay for an occupation has been shown to decrease when women start entering the field in larger numbers.[6] In other words, any occupation that begins to employ more women than men will pay lower wages, and vice versa. Computer programming, for example, was once a job considered menial labor and held mostly by women, but once men began entering the field, it became prestigious and the salaries increased.

How does this affect us as fundraisers? Besides the fact that is inequitable, living on a low salary can mean not realizing dreams, staying in bad relationships, not leaving dead-end jobs, and families making do with less. That can also mean that when the pressures of the job become overwhelming, the addition of the financial stress is enough to make a great fundraiser quit.

I remember the feeling of exasperation when my male colleague who was many years my junior was promoted to the same director level position as me, despite having far less experience or credentials. Our male CEO simply said that this junior colleague, "reminds me of myself when I was younger," and promoted him, despite the fact that he had only a bachelor's degree and a few years of experience, while I had multiple advanced degrees and over a decade and a half of experience. I remember asking exactly what criteria one needed to get promoted, if this colleague could be promoted so easily, because perhaps the same could be possible for me? My boss laughed and told me that in my case, I would have to wait until someone retired or died. (Insert the exasperated eye-rolling emoji here.) This is the reality of sexism our workplaces.

At the same time, because the majority of nonprofit employees, including fundraisers, are women, they are expected to do more with less. They are expected to wear multiple hats and perform multiple jobs. If you are responsible for fundraising, chances are that you are also expected to create the communications and messaging for the fundraising, plan events for funders to attend, coordinate any donor travel or site visits, and handle the proverbial, "other duties as assigned." I see fundraising job descriptions all the time that are asking for three roles in one and are paying the same starting salary that I made twenty-five years ago, before inflation.

And yet, even while juggling chainsaws on fire – meeting with donors at their private club, planning a donor cultivation house party, also planning an annual gala and auction, drafting copy for donor emails and letters, preparing your CEO for a meeting with important donor prospects, etc. – women are told that they are not good enough to hold an executive leadership position. Even when they are asked to take on multiple roles, society believes their work is less important and less valuable. Just like in the poorest countries in the world, when there is not enough to go around, the women and girls eat last.

These myths are damaging because they shift the blame from systemic issues of patriarchy and white supremacy to us. In other words, our institutions are failing us, and we have been told that it's our fault. We are told that we should not complain, but should play the good girl and follow the rules (even though the rules weren't created by us or for us).

Just keep playing by the rules and maybe someday you'll be rewarded. Do you really need a better salary? Women can't be trusted with money, anyway, so what good would a higher salary do? Women are bad at math, women are so frivolous with all those shoes they buy, and anyway, money is dirty so you don't want it because it will affect your purity. Better to just let the men handle it. You should just be grateful for a salary at all.

These gender dynamics also extend to the board of directors, who have an important role to play in an organization's fundraising. Boards, as a whole, also suffer from the same race and gender diversity issues, because people invited to join a board are often invited based on their ability to support the organization's work financially and to open doors to their friends and networks who can do the same. Historically, the people who have held the most resources are white men. And unfortunately, boards often do not know how to support the work of fundraising, nor are they made accountable for doing so. The UnderDeveloped report showed that 36 percent of nonprofits had no fundraising committee to support their fundraisers, and 17 percent said their boards had no involvement in fundraising at all. All too often, this leads to a nonprofit pinning all their hopes on one person – the fundraiser – without the necessary support for that fundraiser to succeed. And when unrealistic fundraising goals are created by board members from the private sector who have not worked in a nonprofit themselves, who do not represent the people or communities the organization is helping, and who are used to working with the resources afforded to white men in the business sector, the result is a set of overly optimistic goals that are totally out of alignment with reality and can decimate morale.

Is it any wonder that so many fundraisers burn out and quit?

PRACTICING RECONNECTION WHEN WE ARE DISCONNECTED

The antidote to countering myths that make us feel small and disconnected from our power is to first understand that these myths create standards that are both impossible and unreasonable. They were created long ago to uphold patriarchy and white supremacy, and they reinforce the idea that some people hold power, others do not, and that we must prove ourselves to the people holding power in order to share it. They disconnect us from the inherent power we all have, and make us doubt ourselves. When we try to conform to these norms, we exhaust ourselves seeking the approval of those with power. We do endless extra tasks, getting coffee for the meetings, taking the notes, coming in early to set up, staying late to clean up. Unfortunately, these myths have worked their way into our subconscious beliefs and need to be detoxed. We need to flip the script.

Many of us have not fully explored our own subconscious beliefs about our worth. Yet every one of us carries these subconscious beliefs, and they can silently sabotage our fundraising efforts without us knowing. As fundraisers, we are also working with money, and the history in this country of who holds wealth is inextricably tied to our history of colonization, slavery, and wealth hoarding. Laws were created to ensure that some people had access to it, and others did not. Some people were paid fairly for their labor, others were not. Some people were given the right to own and inherit property, and others were considered property. Some people were given access to banks to grow their wealth, and others were not. Over time, this wealth became concentrated, as it was passed down through generations and compounded, and it shaped who we see as successful.

Even if you know this history and are working to decolonize your practices, this shared history lives in our subconscious. It also lives in our philanthropic sector, where $80 billion in assets is sitting, unmoved, gaining interest in private accounts. Only 8 percent is moving to communities of color, and only 2 percent is moving to nonprofits that specifically focus on the needs of women and girls. When we see where the money is moving, we can subconsciously equate that with the value and importance of those people and those issues. If we share those identities, we can equate that with the value and importance of ourselves.

Although money itself is neutral, it is still deeply personal. Each of us has a money story that carries feelings of guilt, shame, and fear. If we did not have enough money, we may carry stories of lack, of our parents fighting about resources, of going without, of fear. If we had too much money, we may carry stories of fear that we might lose it, that people only love us because of our money, that without it we will lose our identity. These money stories also live in our subconscious.

Why am I talking about our subconscious minds in a book about fundraising? Because while we may think that our day jobs are completely separate from our own feelings and belief systems, we simply cannot compartmentalize that way. Our brains do not work this way. And to build the most powerful fundraising partnerships to fund the change you want to see in the world, you need to be a fully embodied fundraiser. That means becoming conscious of the messages you have internalized about your self-worth being equal to your compensation, or that women deserve to earn less. It means becoming aware of all the times you were told that women aren't good with money. It means paying attention to any beliefs you hold that money is dirty, that you yourself could never have it, that people who hold it are corrupt, or that – as I have been told many times – that fundraising is a "necessary evil."

Once you become aware of these messages living rent-free in your subconscious, you need to detox them. Consider how often you upgrade the software on your computer or phone to get rid of the bugs or information that is outdated and no longer works. When was the last time you upgraded your subconscious programming and examined your beliefs?

The thing we often forget is that *our subconscious mind governs 95 percent of our decisions.* (You read that right.) So, reconnecting with our subconscious minds and seeing what's rumbling around in there is much more important than it may seem.

I am a big believer in both meditation and journaling, which have been transformational practices for me. If meditation or journaling is not your jam, you can try taking a walk in nature, sitting somewhere you find calming while answering these questions in your mind, or typing them wherever you like to keep notes. The important thing is to take a few minutes to quiet your mind (*not* while you are multi-tasking: writing donor acknowledgment letters, entering your notes from a donor meeting into SalesForce, planning for your annual gala, etc.) and ask yourself these questions.

REFLECTION QUESTIONS

1. What is your own money story in your family lineage? Do you carry a feeling of lack or a fear of not having enough? How might this influence the way you approach your work?
2. Have you ever been aware of salary differences in your workplace based on gender? What feelings arise from feeling like you are not being paid what you are worth? How might this influence the way you approach your work?
3. Have you ever compared yourself to a peer who makes a higher salary? What kinds of stories do you tell yourself about their life? What kinds of stories do you tell yourself about your own worth and capabilities?
4. What words come to mind when you think about money? (e.g., shame, fear, uncertainty, or power, strength, independence?) What words come to mind when you think about wealth? Are they the same?
5. What does it feel like when you ask a donor or donor prospect for money? What feelings does it

provoke? (e.g., fear, anxiety, gratitude, or joy?) How are those feelings connected to your own sense of worth?

Becoming aware of the subconscious programming we have picked up – from society, our families, and our workplaces – is the first step to reconnection. Now we need to clean out those old beliefs we've been told and replace them with new programming. Re-wiring our subconscious beliefs requires identifying our limiting beliefs – the exercise we just did – and them replacing them with empowering beliefs. Affirmations and visualization are one of the best ways to do this. Every thought you think strengthens the circuitry in your brain known as your neural pathways. The more you think a thought, the easier and more automatic it becomes to think that thought. So begin to notice when these limiting beliefs arise, repeat to yourself more positive beliefs, and notice the gradual effect they have on how you approach your fundraising.

AFFIRMATIONS

- The world is abundant, and there is more than enough funding for all of our organizations.
- I am worthy of receiving limitless abundance.
- What I seek is seeking me. My dream donors are out there looking for me to introduce them to my nonprofit.
- My success is not dependent on the approval of those in power. My success is my birthright.
- There will always be people who will criticize me and have something to say. I choose to believe in myself regardless.

- I hold the power to alchemize money into transformation.
- I am constantly creating opportunities for donors to partner with me.
- I am a magnet for dream donors to support my vision of a better world.

5

CONNECT TO YOUR SELF: LETTING GO OF SCARCITY MINDSET

"We are showered every day with gifts, but they are not meant for us to keep. Their life is in their movement, the inhale and the exhale of our shared breath. Our work and our joy is to pass along the gift and to trust that what we put out into the universe will always come back."

— ROBIN WALL KIMMERER

It's no secret that a sense of scarcity pervades the nonprofit sector. This sector is literally defined by what it is not – *not an* organization that creates a profit and has surplus resources. The result? A culture of scarcity that can breed competition rather than collaboration. It means that we become used to making do with less than we need, going without, and working in a culture that tells us we should take whatever we can get, even if we are incredibly uncomfortable with the donor or the source of their wealth.

Here are some of the ways I have seen this manifest in my work and with my clients.

COMPETITION OVER RESOURCES

Often nonprofits compete with one another for grants, believing there is not enough to go around for everyone, including a scarcity of resources for salaries, for consultants that can help when organizations are short-staffed or need specialized expertise, and not enough to budget for mental health and wellness time.

This competition mentality is not only harmful for movement building – because our organizations could do much more by working together than by competing with one another – it is also harmful because it often pits staff against one another. This is especially true with any employee who is a minority in their organization, primarily women and people of color, who have been made to believe that there is only one seat at the table for us.

Healthy competition is not the same as rivalry. I have experienced this throughout my career, but never was it more painful than when a woman and fellow colleague I was working with became jealous and plotted behind my back to sabotage my work so that she could take my job. There was, in truth, an abundance of resources and plenty for both of us to thrive. If she had talked with me about her desires for a different role, I would have loved to brainstorm with her and explore the possibilities to create a new role where we both succeeded and supported one another. Instead, she was operating from a scarcity mindset, believing there was only enough for one of us. This divide and conquer mentality pits us against one another as competitors, rather than as collaborators. Because my colleague believed there could only be one seat at the table and it was either her or me, she sabotaged my work to take the job for herself, and simultaneously secured a lucrative contract for her husband whom she directly supervised. What could have been a win-win for everyone ended up costing the organization dearly, as she was unable to work with other women in the organization either and eventually left to start a competitor organization. Funders were confused and pulled in two directions, and the drama detracted from the work we were all trying to accomplish.

ASKING FOR LESS THAN YOU NEED

The culture of scarcity also comes from donors who may not fully understand how nonprofits operate or who may be misinformed about the true costs of doing their work and impose funding restrictions. There has been much written about the trend (plague?) of donors refusing to pay for a nonprofit's overhead costs, which has caused countless damage to nonprofits who must once again do more with less. Those costs may be asking staff to take on additional work without any additional compensation, working in substandard conditions (I have worked on so much broken furniture and outdated computers that it hurts to recount it – there's nothing like working on a grant proposal on a rustic, old laptop and suddenly seeing the blue screen of death), and fostering a culture of overworking and toxic productivity because there isn't enough staff available to fill in when someone needs time off. I have seen so many grant agreements that included ridiculous overhead restrictions out of a misguided assumption that a nonprofit's success lies in its ability to perform miracles based on tiny amounts. *What an incredible organization, with only $200 they had seven employees run a program for a month!*

In his book *Unicorns Unite*, nonprofit expert and hummus enthusiast Vu Le describes these donors as "overheadholes." He defines overheadholes as, "A person, nonprofit, or foundation who is obsessed with low overhead. They reinforce the idea that any organization that has 'high' overhead is terrible and ineffective, with immoral staff who hoard money for themselves and who have bad personal hygiene and never call their mothers." Although this overhead myth has long ago been debunked (you may have seen Dan Palotta's TED Talk, "The Way We Think About Charity is Dead Wrong," that went viral several years ago), many a donor still believes that there is some correlation between a nonprofit's impact in the world and how much they spend on their rent, lightbulbs, and paying their staff a fair living wage. Even though successful businesses have an average overhead rate of 25 percent, with some industries such as technology at 40- 50 percent, and even though there are no standardized industry-wide metrics for evaluating overhead rates, donors are still obsessed. When I hear a philanthropist client cite the percentages a nonprofit spends on their overhead vs their programs as their rationale for funding them, I know I have a lot of work to do with that client to help them detox these myths and think about meaningful impact differently.

The unintended consequence is that nonprofits, believing they must cater to their donors or risk losing their funding, do everything possible to reduce their overhead, often at the cost of the wellbeing of their employees. It may also mean that fundraisers may be told not to ask for what the organization really needs, forcing them to create a fictional narrative about the true costs of social change. This means that nonprofit employees, and especially women and people of color, continue to be paid less while they are expected to do more. It means that nonprofits may not be able to hire people with disabilities who require special accommodation. It means that employees are often asked to wear multiple hats and take on multiple roles. Since few nonprofits budget for their employee's mental health and wellbeing, the exhaustion from wearing so many hats can lead staff to burn out or quit.

TAKING MONEY FROM SHADY FUNDERS

All too often, a scarcity mindset is reinforced when we receive the message from our leadership that under no circumstances can we turn down money – we must take any donation we can get. As a result, we can find ourselves in uncomfortable and unethical situations with donors who are really not in alignment with our values, or who misuse their power because they know that they hold the money, and we need the money. In my experience as a consultant and coach, these uncomfortable situations with donors and the ethical dilemmas they present can eat us alive from the inside. More often than working too many hours or not reaching a fundraising target, it is the mental and emotional havoc wreaked by these inequitable power dynamics that leads fundraisers to burn out and quit.

There have been countless times when I was working in a nonprofit and a donor approached the organization in a way that made me incredibly uncomfortable. Earlier in my career, I was asked to meet with older male donors because the leadership thought it might be more effective for that donor to meet with a young woman in a short skirt. It was incredibly creepy, and I did not feel that I could say no, because my job was on the line and I cared about the organization's mission. On more than one occasion, I found myself with a lecherous older donor and worried that if I had to fight him off with a plastic fork from the buffet table, I would be fired.

I have also been in situations where a donor has insisted on a quid pro quo for their donation, such as a seat on the board of directors, or hiring their child / nephew / niece as an intern. (Once, a donor's son secured an internship and on their first day of work told an inappropriate sex joke. Although every woman in the organization stayed a hundred feet away from him for the remainder of his internship, we knew there was nothing we could do because his presence was required to satisfy the donor. Unfortunately, one of our most brilliant and talented interns quit because she couldn't stomach working with him.)

I have also been in situations where a donor made homophobic comments and I was told not to take it personally, because, *"They're just from another generation,"* and in situations where a donor threw a temper tantrum and literally yelled and banged his fists on the table while telling the staff they were stupid. And, on more than one occasion, I have discovered that a donor was physically abusive to his wife and the police were called.

These situations caused me so much mental anguish that I lost sleep, had to seek counseling, and eventually quit, because I could not justify working to advance social justice and equity while taking funding from people that were causing harm with impunity.

My stories are not unique. I know that many of you are nodding right now as you are reading this, and if you have experienced these things too, you are not alone. I have also heard similar stories from my nonprofit clients who have shared stories of donors being so verbally abusive to them that they left their meeting in tears, or had donors refuse to participate in Diversity, Equity, and Inclusion (DEI) training and then make harmful comments that hurt staff who were people of color, LGBTQIA+, or had a disability. All of these fundraisers felt they must put up with this abuse because the donor held the funding that was vital to achieving their mission.

This is the danger of a scarcity mindset, and unfortunately, it is ubiquitous in nonprofit culture. As fundraisers, we may see more than our fair share, because we often need to recount stories of scarcity among our target communities in order to make the case that our organizations need funding. We tell these stories over and over to donors and prospects, repeating the lack – the lack of protection, the lack of attention, the lack of access, and the lack of rights in our communities and our planet. These messages of scarcity, as you might guess, can become reinforced in our subconscious.

SCARCITY IN PHILANTHROPY

Scarcity mindset is not only rampant in our nonprofits – it is rampant in philanthropy writ large, though it manifests differently. This might seem strange, since we tend think of foundations as the holders of infinite wealth with a surplus of resources, but as a society we are all surrounded by these narratives. The very reason that wealth is hoarded is because of a belief that resources are finite and that they need to be stockpiled to protect our survival. In the financial sector, wealth advisers view their role as protectors, and they are trained to protect their clients from giving too much way. That means that decisions about how much funding should be allocated to nonprofits are made with these narratives about scarcity in mind.

As a philanthropic advisor, I have had many conversations with funders about what they perceive as "too much" or "not enough" investment in a particular social issue. I have had clients grapple with concerns that they might be giving too much to Black women and not enough to Indigenous women. I have had clients write their biggest checks to protect access to reproductive health care, and instead of being celebrated they were reprimanded by their family for being reckless. All of these prompted interesting conversations about where our feelings of "enoughness" come from, what triggers our feelings of scarcity, and how thinking about these issues intersectionally makes it impossible to disconnect one issue from another.

So often in philanthropy, we break down our work into separate "issue areas" when they are, in fact, all connected. As a fundraiser, you have likely been told at some point by a funder, *"Sorry, we do not fund your issue area,"* even when you brilliantly explained how the issues and organizations they fund directly connect to your work. It becomes difficult to say, *"Actually, the housing issues we are addressing are not really about zoning, but about racial equity and LGBTQ rights. The maternal mortality goals we are addressing are actually about racial equity and xenophobia in our healthcare systems. The climate change goals we are tackling are really about indigenous sovereignty and environmental racism."* Instead, we fill out the grant applications as specified and do our best to write in a way that caters to what we know about the donor's preferences after obsessively Googling them to find out their pet's name and their favorite vacation spot.

As a sector, we know restricted grants and one-year gifts run counter to the long-term, flexible support that is needed to make real progress. Pervasive social challenges such as climate change, access to healthcare, and food security cannot be solved by one organization, with one grant, in one fiscal year. First, it does nothing to advance the bigger goals we are trying to reach as a movement by thinking small. These issues are interconnected and woven together, and to address only one piece of them is like trying to solve a toxic spill in the ocean by mopping up only one area of the shore.

Second, this siloed approach misses crucial opportunities for learning and building authentic relationships. When I look back at the most rewarding relationships I have had with donors, it is always the funders that have engaged in difficult conversations and been willing to dig into hard questions.

To create real change, both fundraisers and donors have to be willing to try new solutions. We have to take risks. (More on that later.) We already know that the way we have been doing things thus far has produced these results. To continue doing them and expecting different results is the definition of insanity.

FROM SCARCITY TO ABUNDANCE

We are living in unprecedented times. During these last several years, as we have grappled with a once-in-a-century global pandemic, a presidential administration that unraveled the safeguards protecting the wellbeing of our communities, and a long overdue racial reckoning, the philanthropic sector has been grappling with its role. There has been an undeniable recognition that the philanthropic sector needs to move away from the historically white, male-dominated power structure it has held since the sector was created to a way of operating where power is shared equally by all.

So many of us working in nonprofits to support communities on the frontlines became worn down, disoriented, and numb. We experienced one crisis after another with no rest or relief, because once we addressed one disaster – the Kavanaugh confirmation hearings, the family separation policy that put children in cages, the record number of anti-LGBTQIA+ legislation and attacks on the queer community, etc. – we barely had time to catch our breath before the next crisis.

This is a time when nonprofit and philanthropic leaders alike need to smash silos (Hulk smash!) that keep nonprofits and our interconnected issues pitted against one another for funding. We need to remember that our suffering and thriving is mutual, and so, too, are funders and fundraisers. Today, we are working in separate rooms, talking about the exact same issues. These walls that separate us – keeping nonprofits apart, and keeping nonprofits and funders apart – are inhibiting the opportunity for critical conversations about how to work together to solve our common challenges.

Our scarcity mindsets have convinced us for too long that we do not hold the power to change things. We have listened to the limiting beliefs that have kept us in our place and have told us that there was too much risk to ask for more. *Conversations that alienate donors could get you fired. If you must address them, be sure not to make the donor uncomfortable. Maybe you can disguise racial and gender justice behind more neutral language like "community initiatives."*

Whether we have experienced repercussions or we have witnessed it happening to colleagues when pushing back against a funder, we are holding a limiting belief that we will not be safe if we object, ask for more, or suggest a new way to fund multiple issues together. We have become disconnected from our power and convinced that we should play by the rules, not rock the boat, and not risk upsetting the donors that provide the resources we need. But what happens when we do?

What if we actually did hold the power to change things all along? What if we shifted the way we think about our work to an abundance mindset, looking at all the resources we do have in our networks, and all the people who could be our champions? What if we mapped out all of connections we have, beyond those with financial assets, and considered the abundance of people who support you, let you cry in their office, send you cat memes, and offer new perspectives? What if one new board member was all that was needed to believe in you, rally the troops behind you, and become your greatest fundraising ally? What if the funds you needed appeared unexpectedly, as they did for my organization when it received that mystery call? When it comes to re-wiring our minds, seeing it can help us to believe it.

Last year, students graduating from a historically Black college in Texas arrived at their graduation ceremony to learn that an anonymous donor had paid off each of their student loan balances and they were all debt-free.

A few years ago, the Groundswell Fund, a BIPOC-led reproductive justice organization, talked with thousands of donors and foundation staff to urge them to expand their giving to reproductive, racial, and gender justice for collective liberation. While some donors were put off by being asked to give in this way, the majority of donors were happy to engage in a respectful conversation that pushed their thinking about how they used their philanthropy, and they ultimately funded Groundswell's work.

Or consider the recent donations made by MacKenzie Scott, who inherited billions in her divorce from Amazon.com founder Jeff Bezos and is steadily working to empty the safe and redistribute the money back to the community. Already, Scott has given away $3.8 billion to 465 nonprofit organizations through multi-year, unrestricted, general operating gifts. (A fundraiser's dream!) None of these organizations reached out to her to solicit these life-changing donations—they were all surprise gifts, mostly to groups fighting for equity or to under-resourced organizations that are often overlooked by philanthropy.

What if you believed the impossible is possible?

Nonprofit fundraisers, this is your time. We ride at midnight.

REFLECTION QUESTIONS

1. Have you ever been in a situation where you felt discomfort with a donor, or were forced to accept their money even though you were not in alignment with them? How did this make you feel?
2. Have you ever turned down a donor interested in funding you? Why or why not?
3. Have you ever felt as though you were being pitted against another colleague or peer organization because there was only enough for one of you? How did that make you feel?
4. When you meet with a donor, do you feel empowered to ask for the resources you actually need? Do you feel that you can ask them hard questions about how much they are giving or the way they are giving?
5. Do you approach conversations with donors thinking about what you need, or what gifts you can offer them by partnering with you?

AFFIRMATIONS

- There is an abundance of resources and more than enough for all of us.
- Donors are interested and excited to engage with me to push their thinking about what could be possible.
- We can do more together than we can alone.
- Right now, there are donors looking for help, and I am the perfect person to help them.
- When I engage in challenging conversations about funding, I am helping everyone move forward.
- I already have everything that I need to attract the resources for my organization.

6

CONNECT TO YOUR PURPOSE

"Such as I am, I am a precious gift."

— ZORA NEALE HURSTON

To work in social change requires the tenacity to know that we are part of a much larger timeline, one that may take generations. It can feel as though we are taking one step forward, two steps back, especially because we are up against systems of capitalism, white supremacy, and patriarchy.

When we get beaten down, it helps us to have an anchor – a deep connection to our purpose for doing this work. Having a true understanding of our purpose helps us to stay the course when waters get choppy, or to know when to listen to the call to move in a different direction.

There will always be a need for fundraisers as long as we live in a capitalist economy where nonprofits remain independently funded. But our purpose goes beyond our current job description, and it will keep us focused when we become exhausted and numb to the work because we know that we are doing it for a greater reason than a paycheck.

When I talk about your purpose, I don't mean in the cliché, "Lifetime Special" sense. It's not the same thing as having a goal, and it's not the same thing as finding the meaning of life. It is about naming what is personally meaningful and what motivates you in a way that focuses your energy toward a larger vision. Over time, our roles will change, but our purpose anchors us and can help us stay balanced.

The reason this is important is because people who identify as being connected to a greater sense of purpose have greater satisfaction in their work, stronger mental health, and better physical health. In other words, being connected to a deeper sense of purpose is something you fully embody that extends beyond your job to your wellbeing. I have found this with my clients as well, even when they come to me in tears, completely overwhelmed.

One client who had recently taken a role as executive director in a small nonprofit found her purpose in bringing more women of color into the organization though its programs and its leadership. Although that was not her job description, this purpose kept her motivated to continue the work even when it was incredibly challenging. Another client, who was a philanthropist, found her purpose in amplifying unheard voices: using her influence and networks to help voices be heard in new places.

My own purpose is something deeply personal to me as well. I believe in gender equality and I work to advance that vision by mobilizing support for women and girls to have the rights and resources they need to thrive. In my professional career, I have done this inside nonprofits working to expand access to financial services for women, advance land rights for women, or strengthen laws for women. I have also done this as a grant-maker and a donor advisor helping to move more philanthropic resources to women and girls. While my roles were different, they all provided different ways that I can enact my purpose through different roles in the ecosystem.

Connecting with your purpose is also important because so often our professional roles and identities become blurred. Many clients have come to me at a crossroads in their career, unsure of who they are without the cloak of their title and their association with that organization. It can be hard to remember that we are so much more than our jobs.

One of my favorite thinkers on this, Deepa Iyer, created a visual map of the social change ecosystem and the different archetypes that we play[1]. I love this imagery of archetypes, rather than professional fields or job titles, because it is so much more expansive. It also reminds us that we may play multiple roles, sometimes simultaneously, and that our roles will likely change or evolve over time depending on what is most needed and where we are in our own lives and in society. The ten archetypes she names are: Guides, Weavers, Experimenters, Frontline Responders, Visionaries, Builders, Caregivers, Disrupters, Healers, and Storytellers. Archetypes like these, used in storytelling traditions around the world, speak to us through timeless and universal patterns about the human experience. Each of us encounters a quest (for example, to raise $5 million to build housing for unhoused residents in our community), which calls for us to rise up (for example, by bringing new funders together to build said housing) and in so doing, discover who we are (brilliant and badass fundraisers who can summon the resources needed to complete the quest). Each archetype bears its own unique gifts, which can help you to understand your purpose in a new light.

To be clear, it is not a prerequisite to fully understand and embody your purpose to be a successful fundraiser in a way that doesn't cause you to become overwhelmed and burned out. That is not the message here. If you don't have a clear sense of your purpose, you are not alone. According to an article by an associate professor of organizational behavior at Harvard Business School, fewer than 20 percent of leaders have a strong sense of their own individual purpose[2]. Sometimes our purpose is revealed slowly by doing the work. To borrow from adrienne maree brown's seminal book *Emergent Strategy*, "less prep, more presence."[3] In other words, sometimes we need to spend less time preparing, or over-thinking, and more time simply being present and open to the manage possibilities that may emerge.

If anyone reading this book has ever been to one of my parties, you probably know that my basement is filled with several Tupperware bins of costumes, and I love to bring them out and lay out the many sparkly, bizarre options when people gather. Inevitably, as people are excitedly trying on fake moustaches and funny hats while cackling, I will hear someone pick up an item – a feather boa, a disco ball headband, a gladiator muscle chest, LED flashing hair extensions, etc. – and exclaim, "Oh, this is *you!*" and place an item on another person and marvel. There are oohs and ahhs and laughter and sometimes a cat-walk strut as the person admires their new look.

It is our nature to try out new identities and make new discoveries about ourselves. Perhaps we have revealed or learned something unexpected about ourselves? *I feel like Tina Turner when I wear sequins.* Perhaps we have confirmed something we secretly believed? *Men really should wear more dresses.*

Our jobs are like these costume pieces, and we can wear different pieces or change them if we discover that wearing the rainbow tutu or enormous moustache is scratchy, is cutting off the circulation to our waist, or that it is downright painful. I recognize the privilege in being able to change jobs, when many of us struggle to find work. What I want to highlight here is that the core of our purpose for *why* we do fundraising work in a nonprofit goes beyond the particular nonprofit job description we hold.

Sometimes, when I ask clients and colleagues about their purpose for doing this work and what keeps them in the work when it is hard, they confuse this question with their life's purpose. I hear responses like, "My purpose is to be a good mom to my daughter Charcuterie." (Note: I don't have any client's names in this book, and any resemblance to a client who named their child after a meat and cheese snack board is purely coincidental.) It is possible that there is strong overlap between your life's purpose and your work, but for most, they are not exactly the same thing. The reason that you get out of bed in the morning or the reason you chose to incarnate in this body during this particular place and time on earth is probably not the same as the reason you feel called to do fundraising work for your nonprofit. You could have chosen any number of careers, all of them probably more lucrative financially, but something inside you led you to choose a role that is meaningful to you in some way. That is important to how you see yourself contributing to your community and to the world.

Not everyone cares about contributing to society, changemaker. Not everyone would put their values –

protecting the earth, ending gun violence, helping survivors of violence heal and get back on their feet – before their income. This is not about judging whether one is better than the other – we all understand the need to take care of our families. But this choice to do this work is intrinsically part of what makes you special. Without people like you, there would be more suffering in the world.

There are times when work in the nonprofit sector feels thankless, exhausting, and never-ending. The problems we choose to tackle – poverty, homelessness, climate change, gender inequality, racial inequality, etc. – are so immense and the issues so complex that it is easy to feel beaten down and exhausted. Connecting to your purpose, while not a silver bullet for all of the harm caused by systems of capitalism, patriarchy, and white supremacy – is an important reminder that we can be part of bending the arc of change. That our efforts do matter.

It can be easy to become overwhelmed by thinking we will never succeed in our lifetimes at solving these problems, even if we spend our days inspiring people to support the work. It is important to remember that small victories are what lead to monumental changes. Each of us is one set of footsteps in the long march forward, but we can create our own visions of success and define what it means for us. In other words, defining success for ourselves, not just for our organizations, invites you to think about how you spend your time doing something that matters to you. Success might look like helping to create a nonprofit sector that is deeply revered and valued. Success might look ensuring that every employee, volunteer, and donor you touch is honored for their authentic efforts to be better humans and create a safer and more just society. Success might look like finding joy in being a connector or a network weaver who links people who typically do not interact or would not have met. Success might look like intentionally using your gifts of inspiring people through your words to share the opportunity to invest in under-resourced leaders. Or, success might be very specific about an issue you care about, regardless of the role you play – protecting trans youth, disrupting the school to prison pipeline, or protecting elephants from extinction.

Your purpose is unique and authentic to you, and it can change and evolve. Whatever your purpose, and wherever you are in the journey of naming it, connecting to something bigger is important in carrying us through the moments when our jobs feel overwhelming. Your purpose is not only to identify x number of major donors, win x number of grant proposals, and raise x number of dollars for your mission. You are so much more.

Each of us brings something special to the work, and one never knows who a funder will connect with or what powerful ideas will emerge. Once, when I was new in my job, our Development Director called me into a donor meeting completely out of the blue. She had been talking with this donor and had learned they were very interested in microcredit, and because the Development Director knew that I had written my master's thesis on microcredit, she invited me in to meet the donor. There was nothing I needed to prepare – I simply showed up as my authentic self and connected with the donor about my purpose and passion for helping women who were considered invisible and unbankable gain access to the formal economy.

Similarly, connecting with our purpose can help us to know when to stay and when to leave, before we burn out. I have had colleagues and clients recount painful stories of being marginalized, abused, and gaslighted in their work, wondering what to do next. I asked them each whether they thought staying in their current jobs was the best way to live their purpose. Did it give them energy, or did it sap their energy? There are times when we have to muscle through tough challenges and we grow stronger and wiser because of it, and there are times when we suffer unnecessarily and burn out because of myths about toxic productivity and the belief that if we stay and work hard, we will feel a sense of belonging. Connecting with your purpose for doing this work will help determine whether you leave the work vertically or horizontally.

REFLECTION QUESTIONS

1. What issues do you feel most passionate about and how do you see yourself committing to them? Are you connected to them through your current work?
2. How do you want to be remembered? What do you want to be known for?
3. What archetypes do you identify with?
4. How do you see your purpose in relationship to the push and pull of your ego or of society's demands that you play a certain role?
5. What brings you the most freedom and possibility?

AFFIRMATIONS

- I am grateful for continually learning who I am and can be.
- I am a living, breathing example of the kind of world I want to live in.

- I am a powerful force for good in the world.
- I am an alchemist who can play multiple roles in the social-change ecosystem.
- When I allow my gifts to shine, I unconsciously give others permission to do the same.

CONNECT TO COMMUNITY

"The most common way people give up their power is by thinking they don't have any."

— ALICE WALKER

We do the work of fundraising for social change together, not alone.

We do this work inside of nonprofit organizations, movements, and communities. We also do this work inside of systems that are inequitable and slow to change. Just as it is important to remain connected to our purpose for doing this work, it is also vitally important to connect with our community. The COVID pandemic made the importance of being in community more paramount than ever, because each person's actions affected the community, and our resilience depended on one another. It made it undeniable that our suffering and thriving was mutual.

The COVID pandemic exposed in an undeniable way the cracks in all of our systems and structures, particularly with regard to race, gender, identity, and disability. In addition to the medical, economic, and social devastation, we watched the pandemic's disproportionate effects on communities of color and on women and girls, including spikes in domestic violence, a departure of millions of women from the workforce (women accounted for 100 percent of the jobs lost during the month of January 2021), dismal health impacts from a lack of access to sanitary products during menstruation (including infections), and millions of girls being taken out of school worldwide. Since women were on the frontlines of the battle to defeat COVID's spread (70 percent of health care workers are women), they had greater exposure to the virus. All of these things were exacerbated for women and girls of color and women and girls with disabilities. In just the one year of COVID, decades of progress toward gender equality were erased. And in just one year of COVID, the nation's impatience for systemic racism exploded.

By exposing the inequities in our systems and structures, we witnessed an important moment to come together – in small communities and as a global community – to address what needed to change in order to build back better. We had to rely on one another in different ways – from finding toilet paper to getting vaccines – to survive in uncertain times. It was an important moment for us to understand how our sectors need to work together differently, from the charitable sector to the government sector to the business sector, starting by addressing what *wasn't* working. It renewed our understanding of community with a capital C and increased the urgency for some long-needed and difficult conversations.

For those people who were working in the nonprofit sector at that time, it was a time of being in overdrive, working day and night to help communities in need. This was particularly true for nonprofit organizations focusing on equitable access to healthcare (especially for marginalized communities, including undocumented people, LGBTQIA+ communities, and people with disabilities), food banks, support for survivors of domestic violence (many of whom had been forced to cohabitate with their abusers during lockdown), and for organizations working on racial justice. Social distancing was a vital way in which the spread of the virus was limited, but it placed a larger burden on unhoused people (who disproportionately identify as LGBTQIA+), people who are incarcerated, and others with limited space and tight quarters including migrant workers. As these communities suffered disproportionately, there was also a rise in xenophobia, ignorance, and hate crimes against Asian Americans who were blamed for the coronavirus.

There was no opportunity for rest.

One crisis bled into the next, with new COVID variants and new crises almost every week. Like any disaster, there was some immediate relief from an influx of aid and philanthropic donations, and like any disaster, the trendy donations soon dried up as donors turned their attention elsewhere or began to get numb with fatigue. For fundraisers, this kind of funding roller coaster – a sudden influx of rapid-response donations when a crisis grabs the headlines, and then its sudden disappearance as the news cycle changes – is hard to manage, because the problems for communities do not disappear just because the funding has disappeared. Communities hit hardest need mid- to long-term support long after donors have forgotten about the disaster.

COVID exacerbated the overwhelm, the exhaustion, the fatigue, and the depression that employees in the nonprofit sector were already feeling, and dramatically increased the rates of burnout. While burnout affected people in all sectors, nonprofit organizations are particularly vulnerable to it. A recent McKinsey study of burnout among nonprofits likened the sustained stress of COVID for nonprofit employees to deep sea divers.[1] There is only so much time you can spend in a high-pressure environment under water before you need to decompress, or you risk endangering your health.

Further, because of the multiple crises happening simultaneously – a racial reckoning and a global pandemic – many nonprofits working to address racial justice in their communities were squeezed even harder. The sense of urgency was off the charts. In recent years, scholars studying burnout in the antiracism movement in the U.S. have been documenting how the sudden influx of white activists both helped to support the movement, but also complicated the work and contributed to disproportionate burnout among activists of color. While many racial justice nonprofits were appreciative of white activists' willingness to support racial justice work, the behaviors and attitudes of many white activists sometimes inadvertently created more stress than benefit for activists of color. Like anything else, burnout does not affect everyone equally.

Women activists face intensified levels of public ridicule and invalidation when compared with their male colleagues, and racial justice activists of color – because of the way oppression operates even within anti-oppression movements – grew emotionally and physically exhausted coping with the ways white activists carried their privilege into racial justice movements.[2]

HOW PHILANTHROPY RESPONDED TO COVID AND BLACK LIVES MATTER

The high-pressure environment of COVID and racial injustice forced a long overdue conversation about how the nonprofit sector – the frontline organizations who step in to care for their communities in times of crises like these – can be better supported, and the role and responsibility of philanthropy to support it. The philanthropic sector had already begun to hold conversations about its role in systemic racism in a new way just before COVID, so the door was already slightly ajar before COVID kicked it open.

In his groundbreaking book *Decolonizing Wealth*, Edgar Villanueva wrote about how the philanthropic sector has evolved to mirror the same colonial structures of the founding of United States, with internalized oppression among the "house slaves" and the select few people of color who gain access to the "plantation" (philanthropic foundations). The timing of this book coincided with another book that took a critical lens to the philanthropic sector, Anand Ghirdaradas' *Winners Take All: The Elite Charade of Charity*, which exposed how many wealthy elites use charitable giving as reputation-washing, but don't actually fund the organizations that are working to change the status quo. Each of these books contributed to a powerful conversation that exposed some of the most troubling behavior in philanthropy and invited a public dialogue.

At the time that charitable sector began to examine what it had been sweeping under the rug, a long overdue racial reckoning exploded. The murders of George Floyd, Breonna Taylor, and Ahmaud Arbery led the nation to a boiling point of civil unrest, triggering worldwide protests against systemic racism, from our healthcare to our economy to police brutality. When support for the Black Lives Matter movement was galvanized, so, too, was the right-wing backlash. Political leaders fanned the flames of division and the whole nation became engulfed.

Our nonprofits called for philanthropy to step up and meet these challenges and corporate philanthropy also stepped up in a bigger way to answer the call. We saw corporate foundations become more involved in supporting nonprofits and movements, acknowledging the role they play in racial inequity and seeking to support social change through their philanthropy. We saw many corporate foundations promise to take an active role in confronting systemic racism by proclaiming, "Black Lives Matter," on their websites. We also saw many new conversations in philanthropic conferences and in philanthropic media about the urgency of shifting greater funding to racial equity.

How have these conversations changed the way that the philanthropic sector supports nonprofits and the people who power them day in and day out? In truth, with "two steps forward, two steps back." On the one hand, it was heartening to see so many corporate foundations step forward to acknowledge their role in systemic racism, align with the Black Lives Matter movement, and pledge billions of dollars in support. On the other hand, just a few years after these powerful proclamations, the data show that 90 percent of the amount promised by the biggest corporate foundations ($45.2 billion) was never given to nonprofits as grants, but rather as loans they could profit from, such as mortgages. (Two banks, JPMorgan Chase and Bank of America, accounted for most of those commitments.) Of the billions committed, only $70 million was allocated in grants that went to organizations focused specifically on criminal justice reform, the cause that sent millions into the streets protesting George Floyd's murder.

This, too, is a contributor to the rise in burnout.

The seesaw of crisis after crisis, a less-than-stellar response from funders who support this vital work, the complications of white activists and donors engaging in racial justice work and inadvertently replicating racism, the disproportionate burdens placed on women in the home and in the workplace, frustration about the slow pace of social change even in the face of global crises – it became a perfect storm for sheer exhaustion.

This is how we arrived at this moment, with record levels of burnout in our nonprofits, especially among women. How do we find our way through it?

One way to do this is by connecting to one another, in community. It is by remembering that just as with COVID, our resilience is bound up with one another. Just as we must connect to our purpose, we must stay connected to the people who support us, who sustain us, and who remind us who we are. We must remain connected to those we are doing this work for, the people who may have done the least to contribute to the problems but are often the ones who suffer the greatest, and who are not always at the same tables with us. We can be their megaphone. We can stay connected to ourselves and our purpose by centering our communities in our work.

Obviously, this work can feel slow at times. We move at the speed of trust. But as we continue to move forward, celebrating small advances and re-grouping after backpedaling, we can see progress and the importance of remaining focused on and connected to our communities. One of the most significant moments of progress is in the way that the sector talks about, thinks about, and centers leaders in our communities who are closest to the issues we are solving.

Several years ago, I was visiting a grantee partner in northern Brazil, in Fortaleza. It was a nonprofit organization working inside urban slums (*favelas*) where families had been living, somewhat precariously, for generations. These favelas were constructed out of necessity for low-cost housing, but although the residents took great pride and care for their homes, paid their electric bills, etc., few people living in the favelas had any legal paperwork for their residences. Through a legal loophole, the government had the ability to demolish these neighborhoods if residents could not prove their ownership, a legal right few of the residents were aware of. One of the favelas I visited was more than a hundred years old, with multi-generational families living in the same homes. I met a woman named Yope Maria who had lived there since she was a teenager, raising ten children, fourteen grandchildren, and now a great-grandchild. Yope Maria and her neighbors had just learned that their home was set to be demolished and turned into an aquarium for tourists. There were no plans to rehouse the people who lived there, and Yope Maria was understandably nervous – she had watched other favelas disappear under bulldozers.

Fortunately for Yope Maria, even though she and her neighbors felt invisible to the government, a local nonprofit organization stepped in to help, simply because they knew the importance of caring for one another as a community. It was a small and youth-led organization of recent law graduates, communications professionals, and artists, who came together to help the residents understand their legal rights and use social media to document what was happening in order to keep the government accountable.

I thought about this community a lot during the beginning of COVID, and how this small nonprofit had showed up to help these vulnerable residents understand how to navigate complicated government systems when they needed help. It was this small nonprofit that provided a true sense of security and safety for the community, simply by caring for their neighbors. It was not the government providing a social safety net, and it was not a large foundation providing a grant. This favela is no different than the communities where you and I live – we thrive or suffer in community with one another, as a collective. Our safety, and our resiliency, lie in our connection as a community.

FROM DONOR-CENTRIC TO COMMUNITY-CENTRIC

This sounds simple, but is actually much more difficult to embody in practice. This is partly because we have been trained to think in terms of individualism, and to see asking for help as weakness. How do we remain connected to community, when we are afraid to be vulnerable by asking for help? How do we remain connected to one another despite our frustration with the slow pace of change? How do we use our relationships and proximity to foundations to understand and examine how clinging to money for safety will not help us the same way as seeing our safety in the collective care for one another? How do we keep from becoming exhausted by watching corporations steal resources from our communities, undermining our collective future safety?

We do it together, as a community.

There is power in collective action. No person can do everything, but everyone can do something. And the doing something feeds us the vital energy of knowing we did not remain silent in the face of injustice, but acted, however imperfectly. We must continue to chip away at social change while staying grounded in our connectedness, even when we don't know the time horizon for change to happen.

Take heart, changemakers, because your efforts are changing things. Two new movements have emerged in recent years that have demonstrated this shift: trust-based philanthropy and community-centric fundraising. While they share some overlap in their focus on centering community, trust-based philanthropy is designed for funders and community-centric fundraising is designed for nonprofits, each offering a unique framework that contributes to a more just and equitable nonprofit sector.

Launched in January 2020, the Trust-Based Philanthropy Project[3] is a five-year, peer-to-peer, funder initiative to address the inherent power imbalances between foundations and nonprofits. Initially led by Pia Infante at the Whitman Institute, which intentionally spent down all its capital and closed its doors this year, the Trust-Based Philanthropy Project recognizes that philanthropy does not hold all the answers. While many of its practices are not new, there was a desire to build on these practices and create a structure for a growing community of funders committed to making the ecosystem of philanthropy more equitable. At its core, trust-based philanthropy encourages funders to trust communities – the local nonprofits that work in those communities, and the people living in the communities who are in closest proximity to the issues funders are trying to address. This is a vastly different approach than that of many large foundations who hire researchers from the world's most prestigious universities to identify solutions for communities. It is a bottom up, rather than a top-down, approach to partnering with nonprofits to support and sustain their work.

Trust-based philanthropy is designed for mutual accountability between funders and nonprofits, and getting there requires addressing the easy-to-talk-about but hard-to-do power dynamics that underpin the sector, in which the people with the funds get to make the decisions. To cede power and to trust that the people closest to this work know what their communities need is quite revolutionary, considering that most foundations still require a case for support, considerable progress reports, and detailed impact metrics. Instead, trust-based philanthropy explores how our collective social change work might be different if funders approached their relationships with nonprofits from a place of collaboration, rather than compliance and control.

Trust-based philanthropy is implemented though a set of six principles that, when practiced together, help to right-size power imbalances between funders and grantees in order to facilitate deeper, more transparent relationships. They are:

1. *Give multi-year unrestricted funding.* The work of nonprofits is long-term and unpredictable. Multi-year, unrestricted funding gives grantees the flexibility to assess and determine where grant dollars are most needed, and allows for innovation, emergent action, and sustainability.
2. *Do the homework.* Oftentimes, nonprofits have to jump through countless hoops just to be invited to submit a proposal.
3. *Trust-based philanthropy* flips that script, making it the funder's responsibility to get to know

prospective grantees, saving nonprofits time in the early stages of the vetting process.

4. *Simplify and streamline paperwork.* Nonprofits spend an inordinate amount of time on funder-driven applications and reports, which can distract them from their mission-critical work. Streamlined approaches focused on dialogue and learning can pave the way for deeper relationships and mutual accountability.

5. *Be transparent and responsive.* Open, honest, and transparent communication supports relationships rooted in trust and mutual accountability. When funders model vulnerability and power-consciousness, it signals to nonprofits that they can show up more fully.

6. *Solicit and act on feedback.* Philanthropy doesn't have all the answers. Nonprofit grantees and communities provide valuable perspectives that can inform a funder's strategy and approach, inherently making our work more successful in the long run.

7. *Offer support beyond the check.* Responsive, adaptive, non-monetary support bolsters leadership, capacity, and organizational health. This is especially critical for organizations that have historically gone without the same access to networks or level of support as their more established peers.

To be clear, trust-based philanthropy does not mean trusting all nonprofits unconditionally. Everyone who has ever owned a cat or babysat a sneaky two-year old who knows where the cookies are hidden understands that trust must be earned. Rather, trust is the starting point for modeling mutual accountability and the necessary precursor for working through challenging moments when trust is challenged or breaks down. Similarly, all unrestricted funding is not automatically trust-based funding; there has been some debate about whether MacKenzie Scott should be considered a trust-based philanthropist because she practices some of its principles. Taken together, trust-based philanthropy outlines a roadmap for shifting power imbalances in the nonprofit sector by reducing the burden on nonprofits (and especially fundraisers), and communicating to nonprofits that they are valued, trusted, and seen.

Just as trust-based philanthropy is a model for philanthropists to examine how they approach their work, community-centric fundraising is a fundraising model for the nonprofit sector that prioritizes communities and movements over individual nonprofit organizations. Grounded in equity and social justice, the community-centric fundraising movement was created to foster a sense of belonging and interdependence, and to encourage mutual support rather than competition between nonprofits.[4]

The origins of community-centric fundraising came from a frustration in the ways that philanthropy often perpetuates the very injustices they are seeking to end, and often ends up centering the desires of donors rather than centering the needs of the community. In doing this, philanthropy has avoided difficult conversations about race, inequity, and privilege caused by wealth disparities, as most wealth is built on historic injustice. Philanthropy has also perpetuated the othering of communities they serve, describing them as beneficiaries of charity and aid, instead of active partners. This has contributed to a "white savior complex" in which wealthy white donors or foundation executives are saving people in need.

Similar to trust-based philanthropy, community-centric fundraising seeks to address the perception that donors hold the best solutions to injustice, instead of centering the communities most affected by injustice who, because of their lived experience, may have the best solutions. To practice de-centering donors and instead center the communities being served, community-centric fundraising practices ten principles:

- Fundraising must be grounded in race, equity, and social justice.
- Individual organizational missions are not as important as the collective community.
- Nonprofits are generous with and mutually supportive of one another.
- All who engage in strengthening the community are equally valued, whether volunteer, staff, donor, or board member.
- Time is valued equally as money.
- We treat donors as partners, and this means that we are transparent, and occasionally have difficult conversations.
- We foster a sense of belonging, not othering.
- We promote the understanding that everyone (donors, staff, funders, board members, volunteers) personally benefits from engaging in the work of social justice – it's not just charity and compassion.
- We see the work of social justice as holistic and transformative, not transactional.
- We recognize that healing and liberation require a commitment to economic justice.

Taken together, these movements not only complement one another, but are offering frameworks for both nonprofits and funders to take action and be accountable to one another. In addition, another supporting movement among funders called Participatory Grantmaking (PGM), has steadily been building a thriving community of funders who are sharing with one another their efforts to involve communities, nonprofit grantees, and others in the grantmaking process.[5] PGM urges traditional foundations to be more transparent and accessible, and encourages experimenting with inviting community members or other grantee partners to contribute to making funding decisions. Although the practice of PGM itself is not new, the evidence and support for it has been growing in recent years, with large and well-known foundations such as the Ford Foundation showing evidence that it contributes to more equitable grantmaking decisions. Like trust-based philanthropy and community-based fundraising, participatory grantmaking recognizes that funders do not have all the answers, and that power-sharing builds trust and collaboration that is vital for making real progress.

Imagine a future of philanthropy when these practices become the norm and are practiced collectively. When we are open to learning from one another's experiences, it offers a powerful opportunity to find our power in community with one another.

REFLECTION QUESTIONS

1. Where might you strengthen your work by reaching out to a peer or colleague in solidarity?
2. Have you and your team discussed how to hold conversations with your donors about centering

the needs of the community and prioritizing their lived experience? What might that allow for?
3. How have conversations about race shifted in your organization since 2020? How have they shifted among your donors?
4. Have you explored adopting the principles of community-centric fundraising in your organization? How might it be helpful to join this community, or a similar community, to find support, resources, and examples?
5. Have you ever spoken with donors about participatory grantmaking or suggested being part of their grant decision-making process?
6. How might strengthening your organization's equity work strengthen your work overall?

AFFIRMATIONS

- Our suffering, thriving, and liberation is mutual.
- I am always connected to a larger community, even when I cannot see it.
- Someone in the world is having the exact same challenge as me right now, and I can find support through connection.
- I am held by the whole.
- We are all drops in the same ocean.

8

CONNECT TO NOURISHMENT

"Caring for myself is not self-indulgence. It is self-preservation, and that is an act of political warfare."

— AUDRE LORDE

To work in a nonprofit is to constantly be working for change. To work for change means to push against *what is*, in favor of *what could be*. To constantly push requires expending, and then replenishing, your energy. To do this work requires rest.

You may be thinking, *who has time for rest?* I understand that, because we live in a capitalist society and we have been taught that to rest is to be lazy. We constantly see images and messages about hustle culture, grind culture, and the glorification of being busy. *Busy* may be our go-to response when someone asks us how we are doing. We are told that the worst thing we can be is unproductive, and that productivity is tied to our sense of self-worth. These messages live in our subconscious and cause us to work beyond the point of exhaustion until we burn out. I know this because I burnt myself to a crisp, and I will share the wisdom I now know: if you don't choose a time to rest your body, your body will choose it for you.

Let us begin by reframing this idea of productivity that drives many of our decisions. Productivity is not equal to work. The concept of productivity being equal to fulfilling workload quotas is an antiquated concept that originated in cotton plantations in the antebellum South, because slavery was fueling the nation's economy. What if we reframed productivity to mean making intentional choices toward a goal? By reframing productivity as an intentional choice, rest may be the most productive thing we can do.

This is easier said than done, because our collective subconscious is deeply programmed and trained otherwise. But your worth is not based on your work. We can start re-wiring our minds by creating healthy boundaries around how much we work, when we work, and the right balance of rest in order to have the stamina needed to do the meaningful work we are called to do. Like the metaphor of putting on your own oxygen mask first on an airplane before helping others put their oxygen mask on, we must be nourished and rested in order to be of service to others. When we are weary, sleep deprived, unable to be away from our electronic devices without feeling panic, waking up and immediately reaching for our phones, blowing past every personal boundary and feeling guilty about it, we are not bringing our best selves to our donors, our colleagues, or to our communities. As Tricia Hersey, founder of the Nap Ministry says in her book *Rest is Resistance*, *"When we don't take the time to rest for ourselves, while holding the space for others to rest, we are functioning exactly like the systems we want to gain freedom from."*[1]

I bump up against this constantly as a consultant and coach, when clients request my time and assistance but give me last-minute deadlines and expect miracles. Unfortunately, because I was rewarded for pulling off miraculous feats, I became very good at the game of pulling a rabbit out of a hat and became known for doing so with little notice (or compensation). Soon, that became the expectation, not the extraordinary. It was a race to the bottom.

Once I worked with a client that seemed like an absolute dream. It was a prestigious organization that had a famous celebrity spokesperson, and I was giddy at the thought of all that could be possible with that kind of platform to help amplify our message and encourage people to take action. That client happened to be based in another time zone, which is common when you live on the West Coast, and thus our meetings were often very early in the morning, for their convenience.

I would plan my evenings carefully to account for this, knowing I would need to be caffeinated, showered and ready to lead a meeting at 6:30 a.m., so I said no to dinners with friends, asked my wife to take the dog for a walk in the morning, and scheduled my day around these client meetings. It was amazing to me how many times I would be sitting on a Zoom call, notes prepared and ready to go, and just a few minutes before the call started – sometimes even a few minutes after the call should have started – I would receive a message saying, *"Oops, sorry, our previous meeting ran late, do we even need to meet after all?"* This was often followed by a frantic email later that day requesting a new work product with an urgent turnaround. Soon this became a pattern, and when it was time to renegotiate the contract, I chose not to work with them anymore. It was an important lesson for me in standing in my power and setting firm boundaries, even at the risk of losing a client. But in truth I was saying *no* to something that drained my energy, so that I could say *yes* to a more balanced life that replenished my energy. I was saying no to feeling unappreciated and as though my time wasn't valuable, and saying yes to working with clients that were just as excited to work with me as I was to work with them.

To prevent burnout – and to heal from it if you are already there – you need to prioritize self-care like never before. And this is often where we fall short, both as individuals, and as organizations, because capitalism tells us that our worth is directly tied to our work. Without our jobs, our titles, and our roles, it is easy to have an identity crisis. *Who am I, without my title? How do I show society that I am a good person? Do I have any value to society if I'm not serving others and trying to create social change? Does this mean I am giving up? Does this mean that I have sold out?* I know all of these thoughts because I have had them myself, and when I was pushing myself past the point of burnout, I simply could not imagine that people would even recognize me without my nonprofit identity.

When clients come to me with clear signs of burnout, I want to help them begin to heal by restructuring their lives with boundaries that allow them to nourish themselves. This often requires creating time and routines for self-care, to which I am often met with, *"Are you kidding me? Do you know what's on my plate? I don't have time for that."*

I completely understand that objection (pot calling the kettle black, here) but here's the thing: it is much easier to find the time now, before you burn out, to practice healthy boundaries and self-care. It takes much longer to heal from, rather than to prevent, burnout. You will be a more successful leader if you prioritize rest and nourishment. You cannot pour from an empty cup.

To nourish ourselves is vital for our survival, and yet when I talk about self-care I know that many of will roll your eyes and think this is woo-woo. That is fine, because the woo is what will keep you alive and bring you back into balance. Self-care is an act of love. Self-care is an act of resistance against a society that tells you that your worth is only equal to your productivity. Self-care is self-preservation. If you do not care for yourself now, there will be no self to preserve in the future. All we have is now.

Unfortunately, another challenge with a capitalist work culture is that our workplaces shift the burden of burnout to the employee to handle on their own. This happens everywhere, not just in nonprofits, but it is often pronounced in smaller nonprofits because the other staff are themselves overloaded, not because of a desire to escape accountability.

Burnout is *not* an employee problem. It is a symptom of a larger problem in the social change sector, in which the work of nonprofits is vital to society, but so devalued that we don't support any time for employees to take time off and rest.

The objections to taking the time to address burnout as an organization, and as a sector, usually begin with centering wellness and rest. Like investing in overhead (remember the overheadholes?), funders do not want to pay for wellness or anything else that isn't a direct program cost. However, I would counter that if wellness and rest isn't a priority, what *is* a key priority? Can you achieve them without the health and well-being of nonprofit employees and leaders? How much time can you save by responding from a place of being grounded and centered, rather than reacting from a place of stress and exhaustion?

A few years ago, I was working with a research institute funded by a large foundation. I was often asked to prepare PowerPoint decks, strategy documents, and complex workstream spreadsheets, often working late to meet deadlines, only to arrive at the meeting and learn that some new information had made my work irrelevant or there was a completely different and new priority. Somehow, I always found the time to meet the deadlines, but increasingly I found that this came at the cost of having time to exercise, make a healthy dinner, or get enough sleep. I ignored the signs when my cortisol began spiking and I began waking up in a panic at 3:00 am every single day, and then one day I got up from my desk and my back felt like it had snapped in two. I spent the next two months hobbling around, getting my back uncrunched by a chiropractor, and becoming a human pincushion in the acupuncture clinic. As I lay on the table with pins sticking out of me, I realized I had fallen right back into the familiar habit of people-pleasing at the expense of my own health and I vowed never fall to prey to that again.

That (literally painful) experience helped me to remember the importance of prioritizing health and self-care, and now this is core to my coaching work. There is always time. You just need to prioritize it. You will be a more transformative leader if you stop making the excuse that you have no time, and instead take aligned action to move toward a more balanced life.

When it comes to preventing, reversing, and recovering from burnout, there are two powerful sources of inspiration to me that remind me of why rest is so vital. The first is Tricia Hersey's *Rest Is Resistance*, which has four key tenets[2]:

- Rest is a form of resistance because it disrupts and pushes back against capitalism and white supremacy.
- Our bodies are a site of liberation.

- Naps provide a portal to imagine, invent, and heal.
- Our DreamSpace has been stolen and we want it back. We will reclaim it via rest.

These tenets are a reminder to claim our right to rest, and to see it as a way of honoring our power. It is also a reminder to reflect on the importance of rest and to reflect on why we speak so highly of the material things we want or already have to feel expansive without addressing the exhaustion, sleep deprivation, and disconnection we suffer to attain those materials things.

Reading this book prompted me to think about one of my hobbies, ceramics, which I like to do because it engages a completely different and artistic part of my brain, allowing the over-analytic part of my brain to rest and take a load off. (When I say that I do ceramics, you may be imagining the scene from the movie Ghost, but I promise you it is more like mud wrestling with myself while trying to not to splatter clay everywhere.) I find this hobby to be meditative and creative, and yet so often when people learn that I do this they respond by saying, "You should sell your ceramics as a side hustle!" Never have I had an interest in commodifying my creations (which are often new dishes to replace ones that have met with an unfortunate accident) because I see it as a form of relaxation, something I do to put myself into the creative dream state. To create space for yourself to rest, in whatever form that takes, is a powerful opportunity to rejuvenate yourself. It is not a luxury, but a necessity.

The other source of inspiration that has informed my perspective is Sacred Rest by Sandra Dalton-Smith[3], through which I had an insight about how often we conflate rest and sleep, thinking they are the same thing.

We may think we are rested because we have gotten enough sleep the night before, but even after a good night's sleep we are still exhausted. The book speaks directly to those most prone to a lack of rest – high-achieving women, who suffer from a "rest deficit." This is because we don't understand the true power of rest, which is restoration.

Dalton-Smith has a framework to show the seven different forms that rest can take. *Physical rest* is the form of rest we are most familiar with and what we usually turn to when we feel exhausted. However, we may give ourselves extra sleep only to find we still feel exhausted and burnt out when we wake. Passive physical rest is sleeping, while active physical rest could be restorative activities such as yoga or massage therapy that help improve your physical circulation while allowing your mind to rest.

Mental rest is the form of rest we need when we start the day with a huge cup of coffee, but find ourselves struggling to concentrate on our work, and then when we lie down at night to sleep, we struggle to turn off our brains. Despite sleeping seven to eight hours, you may wake up feeling as if you never went to bed. To antidote to a mental rest deficit is to take short breaks every couple of hours throughout your workday to get a change of scenery and move your body. If you can't turn off your over-active monkey mind at night, try keeping a notepad by the bed to jot down any nagging thoughts that would keep you awake.

If you are exhausted by bright lights, computer screens, background noise, and multiple conversations that overwhelm our senses, you might need *sensory rest.* This can be countered by doing something as simple as closing your eyes for a minute in the middle of the day, taking a five-minute meditation break or a short nap, or by intentionally unplugging from electronics to reduce the constant over-stimulation. At the very least, get yourself some blue light glasses to filter out the light you are absorbing form your screens, and whenever possible, get your bare feet on the soil or grass outside.

Creative rest is important for anyone who must solve problems or brainstorm new ideas. Allowing yourself to take in the beauty of nature, listening to live music, or enjoying a new space reawakens the awe and wonder inside each of us. Imagine how differently you will show up to your work if you spend forty hours a week staring at screens, versus immersing yourself in beauty and inspiration that feed your mind with ideas.

Emotional rest means having the time and space to freely express your feelings and cut back on people pleasing. This is vital if you are that person that everyone thinks is the nicest person they've ever met, the one they'd call if they needed someone to dog-sit their ailing, elderly schnauzer who throws up everywhere and requires IV fluids twice a day. When this person is alone, they feel like others are taking advantage of them, but they don't have the energy to respond about how they really feel or they might break down and cry. Emotional rest allows you to answer the question "How are you today?" with a truthful "I'm not okay," and feel safe.

You may need *social rest* if you cannot differentiate between relationships that give you energy from relationships that exhaust you. Social rest can be done by surrounding yourself with supportive people, and limiting interactions with energy vampires (not the cool sparkly ones from Twilight) people who drain your energy when you are around them.

The final type of rest is *spiritual rest,* which allows us to connect deeply to a sense of belonging, love, and acceptance. To receive this, engage in a mindful breathing or meditation practice, spend time in nature, or do whatever provides you with a sense of peace and contentment.

The key takeaways here are that rest is not optional; rest is not an indulgence; and sleeping is not the only way we rest. Physical rest alone is not enough to feel restored. Boundaries around your time are an important part of this equation to ensure that you can take the rest you need to recharge and restore yourself. When you are balanced and rested, you do your greatest work finding the resources to sustain your world-changing work. Connect with what nourishes you.

REFLECTION QUESTIONS

- Have you found yourself asking yourself why you feel so lazy? What if you reframed this to ask yourself, "Why does my body need rest right now? What is the best form of rest?"
- What would it look like to take a day of rest for yourself? What if that day was extended to a week? What would it allow for?
- Of the seven types of rest, which ones speak loudest to you for your own nourishment? Can you see a way to create time and space for them?
- What is one thing you can say no to today that will give you back at least five minutes? How can you use that time to improve your own well-being?

AFFIRMATIONS

- Rest is my birthright. I am worthy of rest.
- Productivity is not working until exhaustion; it is moving toward a meaningful goal that I create.
- I will resist anything that does not center my humanity.
- I am my best version of myself when I take time to pause and breathe deeply.
- Our collective rest will heal the world.

CONNECT TO TRUST: REDEFINING RISK

"Security is mostly a superstition. Life is either a daring adventure or nothing."

— HELEN KELLER

We need to take an honest look at our perception of risk when it comes to investing in the leaders that are on the frontlines of social change. When you think about the greatest heroes who changed the course of history by putting their lives on the line for justice and equity – from Harriet Tubman, to Rosa Parks, to Angela Davis, to Marsha P. Johnson – it is those who had the most to lose and who risked it all for the greater good. Without these heroes, our world would not be the same. And yet, when it comes to supporting courageous leaders and their organizations, too often donors come up with a list of reasons as to why their work is "too risky." I, for one, believe it is completely ass-backward, and that we need to turn this thinking on its head.

Why am I coming out swinging about risk in a book about burnout? It is very difficult to do social change work without trust, which is why I included a chapter on trust-based philanthropy and community-centric fundraising. Trust is core to the work we do, and it is vital to our systems, our organizations, and our relationships with one another. As fundraisers, we know that trust is vital to building meaningful relationships with donors and to bringing them together collectively. Nobody wants to invest in an organization or a leader they don't trust.

Building this trust is vital for another reason: it allows us to innovate when we know that things could be better, or could work differently. And innovation requires taking risks. Can we innovate without having trust first? We can try, but at some point we need someone else to believe in our idea and we need someone to invest in a pilot that allows us to test the idea and see if it actually works. And this is where we often see the say-do gap between what donors say they want —*New ideas! Innovation! Bold action!* — and what they actually do — *I'll only fund it if someone else funds it first.*

As a result, nonprofits can respond to this reluctance by donors to fund new ideas by filtering their creativity and only putting forward ideas they think the donors will like or approve of. It is a dangerous path for all of us when we stifle innovation. It is the definition of insanity to do the same things but expect different results. To change the way things have been, we need to do things that feel unfamiliar and new, and that involves taking risks.

This isn't as easy as it sounds, because although brilliant ideas and talent can come from anywhere (as evidenced by the movie Cool Runnings about the Jamaican bobsleigh team that went to the Olympics), we don't all have the same positional power, and therefore our ideas aren't always heard by leaders and funders. (Or, your idea may be heard, but Chad-the-tech-bro will get the credit for repeating your idea.) We have work to do as a sector, but we also have work to do internally in our own subconscious minds, because our desire to be accepted can interfere with sharing our cool ideas that require some trust and a leap of faith.

So, we are caught in a dilemma: If we share our idea and the donor doesn't fund it, we may be seen as wasting their time, ruining our chances for future funding, or pushing the funder away. If we are *not* taking risks by trying new ideas to make the world better, we are playing small and upholding the status quo. It's people-pleasing at its worst.

When I went to work at the land rights organization and I suggested shining a spotlight on the issue of women's land rights specifically, building off the growing body of research on microcredit and what can happen when women are part of the economy in a whole different way, nearly everyone said no. My boss said no. The program staff said no. The board said no. Even the one researcher who had led the work and authored the research on women's land rights said no at first. They had tried, funders didn't seem interested, and they didn't think it made sense to try again. Imagine how different the world would be if we hadn't taken that risk and put the idea in front of funders anyway?

Not only did we receive more funding than the organization had ever seen by shifting the focus to women's land rights, one of our funders became so convinced that this was a powerful strategy that they created an entire new pillar of their foundation dedicated to funding property rights across the world.

The risk-aversion in philanthropy makes me concerned for the sector, changemakers.

I already have concerns about the collective toll on our psyches when we are afraid to be our full selves in the workplace and we shrink ourselves to "fit in." I don't know about you, but all the greatest rewards I have experienced in my life have followed my greatest risks: interviewing for a job I thought I had no chance in hell of getting, and getting it; asking a funder for a sum of money that made my stomach bounce between nausea and butterflies and hearing them say yes; starting my own business and fearing I wouldn't find any clients, and then discovering my dream clients were waiting for me; and coming out as queer (again) and meeting the woman who would become my wife.

Many years ago, I led a grantmaking program that was doing something quite innovative by investing in small, grassroots projects that typically did not receive funding from U.S.-based foundations. These were small, experimental pilot projects, often ideas that nobody else was funding because they were deemed "too risky." I loved that everything about our approach seemed counter to what traditional philanthropy was doing to fund justice issues.

Typically, when foundations think about the likely recipient of a grant to address justice systems, they invest in the people with deep knowledge of justice systems: lawyers, judges, and law enforcement. We took a totally different approach and invested instead in local community leaders who had been impacted by injustice. We invested in teenage trafficking survivors in Pakistan, women soccer players in Brazil who were barely paid and had no health insurance, and domestic workers in Kuwait whose employers would lock away their phones and force them to work overtime. We invested in these leaders because we believed that improving justice is not simply the job of lawyers any more than improving public health is only the concern of doctors and nurses. To change the "way things have always been done," we decided to invest in the leaders who other funders had deemed too risky.

What does funding risky pilot projects look like? We funded women athletes in Brazil who were tackling gender-based wage discrimination in sports, an industry rife with sexism and double standards, where women athletes were paid minimum wage at best and had no access to health insurance when they were injured, which was frequently given their line of work. They provided training and educational workshops to youth in places where soccer players were most often recruited, helping them to feel safe opening up about gender norms and to learn tolerance and respect.

We funded teenage survivors of sex trafficking in Nepal to become paralegals and work alongside law enforcement to help address the cycle of trafficking among vulnerable girls. We funded tech coders in Argentina who developed an app to allow citizens to see – for the first time – how their elected officials were voting on issues with complete transparency. We funded a radio program in Sierra Leone to translate new laws about women's rights into local languages, so that every woman would know her rights regardless of the language she spoke or whether she could read. We funded these projects because we believed that by inviting new ideas and new people to the table, we would all gain new perspectives and learn from one another.

Was this approach inherently riskier than traditional grantmaking because we invested in unlikely partners? Or was this an underrated approach to encourage innovation and disrupt the way donors often circulate funding only amongst the top organizations? That depends on how you think about risk.

What we learned from this approach is that collaboration with non-traditional partners produced the best results. That is, programs in which lawyers worked with other lawyers or judges were not as successful as the "riskier" programs in which lawyers worked with schools and girl scout programs in Kyrgyzstan to address the problem of bride-kidnapping to help protect teenage girls. Programs where lawyers trained other lawyers were not as impactful as programs where filmmakers in Mexico exposed the way evidence is collected during a suspected crime and used the footage to influence reforms in national criminal policy and procedure. Simply engaging different kinds of partners and utilizing their unique lived experiences tapped different sources of knowledge.

We funded a project in Cameroon considered controversial because local health clinic workers wanted to speak out about corruption in the country's healthcare system, where many citizens were being forced to pay bribes in order to receive basic services such as free diagnosis and treatment of HIV / AIDS, malaria, and other diseases. Through this project, we learned that many healthcare workers were unaware that asking for bribes was extortion – they had simply been emulating the "best practices" (toxic best practices are everywhere) that they had learned from their superiors who told them that bribery was not only socially acceptable, but necessary in order to be good providers for their families. Once the healthcare workers understood the consequences of corruption, their mindsets shifted and their behavior changed. As a result, the country's most vulnerable communities are now receiving better access to healthcare.

In Haiti, we funded a musician-led group to work with lawyers from the entertainment industry to protect their intellectual property rights and negotiate legal contracts with record labels. They held workshops for any interested local musicians that leveraged music industry executives to educate the musicians about IP laws. As a result, not only did local artists improve their business savvy and legal literacy, but their songs about social issues (including pollution, violence, and corruption) had a much wider reach.

We found that these risky ideas led to profound impact, and even when the projects did not succeed, we learned a tremendous amount. Yet when I shared these results with peers in the philanthropic sector, I almost always received the same response: *My boss would never let me do that. That seems risky.* Let's unpack this.

RISKY BUSINESS

In a philanthropic context, risk is relative to begin with, because all money given away for social purposes is effectively gone, regardless of outcomes. Once you give a nonprofit a grant or a donation, you don't see the money again. You receive a tax benefit whether the program succeeds or doesn't. So what, in fact, are we really risking by giving money to charity? Are the risks we take as donors anywhere near the scale of the risks that are being taken by activists and communities and nonprofit organizations? When we, as donors, give $50 to an organization to help refugees forced to flee their homes, and the refugee becomes sick in the camps and does not survive, do we then say that this was not a worthy investment and was too risky?

When I worked as a consultant to the Bill & Melinda

Gates Foundation, I regularly saw investments in the millions going out the door every day to support programs addressing things like better sanitation and health for women in India, or mobile financial services for women living in poverty in Kenya. Did those programs always yield expected results? No program in the world always yields the expected results. We are humans. My client shared that a sanitation project designed to help provide women in agricultural areas have access to better toilets went largely unused, because the women considered anything too far from their home too unsafe to use without the danger of getting assaulted. While it is too bad that programs that don't always work as expected, had the staff at the foundation not invested in that idea, they would not have learned the critical importance of consulting women on the design of such programs from the beginning, greatly improving their future progress and outcomes from that valuable lesson. In my opinion, that grant still had a multiplier effect, because it informed their future work.

First, funders are often mistakenly equating risk as the same in a nonprofit sector as it is in the for-profit sector, and expecting a similar return on investment. This is a very important conversation for fundraisers to have with donors and board members who come from the business sector. We are not comparing apples to apples. Nonprofits are tackling some of society's most stubborn and intractable social issues that are embedded in inequitable laws, policies, customs, behavior, and norms. The time horizon for change is nowhere close to the timeline for turning a profit on manufacturing trail running shoes, and by comparing one to the other, you will always end up with widely disparate results. They simply cannot be compared this way, and to do so is a mistake.

I once was told by my CEO that we would not be sharing the impact report for our grantmaking publicly (despite going cross-eyed crunching all the numbers) because, *"It looked like we had a 50 percent failure rate."* Once I picked my jaw up off the floor, I could only shake my head. This example encapsulates my point here. First of all, if an angel investor had a 50 percent success rate in their investments in small businesses, rather than investing in social justice nonprofits, they would be on the front cover of every finance magazine in the newsstands! Most entrepreneurial business ideas have a 10 percent rate of success. So why do we consider it a risk to invest in the organizations that are tackling our society's greatest and most intractable social challenges? To me, it seems riskier to invest in an entrepreneur who has invented, for example, The Snuggie. (No offense to the Snuggie, and I hope that entrepreneur reinvested the millions they made from that product back into community-led nonprofits.) Imagine how much the nonprofit sector would benefit if we thought of risks and failures in experimenting with ways to solve social challenges as market research?

Second, I think we need to look carefully and honestly at what we are considering "failure" to ensure that we are not conflating failure with risk. There may be many reasons why a nonprofit's program fails. Working in this sector for so many years, I have seen projects fail for myriad reasons. A project in Thailand to monitor human rights in prisons failed when the person bravely serving as the watchdog documented abuse by the police and was threatened and had to abandon the project and leave the country. A project in India to tackle bribery failed because, ironically, the organization was asked to pay a bribe in order for the government to approve their business paperwork so they could receive their grant funding from us.

Another project in India *almost* failed because the local partner suddenly decided that we should scale the project ten times its original size or they were pulling out altogether, and we had to scramble to find more funding and more staff to expand the project.

Consider what the world might miss by not investing in risky new ideas or betting on different types of leader? Years ago, indigenous weavers in Bolivia solved a problem doctors had long been struggling with and nobody in the medical industry could solve. Worldwide, nearly one out of every hundred children is born with a congenital heart disease, often a hole in the heart. The treatment is the insertion of a device called an occluder which closes the hole, but comes with some significant challenges. First, it's difficult to make a device so teeny-tiny and customized to fit the shape of a small child's heart, and second, the device is often neither affordable nor accessible.

The life-saving solution did not come from the medical industry; it came from indigenous women weavers in Bolivia. For the Aymara people, weaving is a tradition deeply embedded in their culture. At a young age, Aymara girls learn a special weaving technique, making their steady hands the perfect solution to create a small, high-tech medical product of much better quality than those that are mass produced in a large factory. Using a single strand of nitinol, the Aymara women carefully weave the tiny occluders (in the shape of a Bolivian hat!) to close the hole in the child's heart. The tiny device can be folded up inside a slim catheter as it travels through blood vessels and is only expanded when it reaches the right place in the heart, recovering its original top-hat shape, and can stay there forever in the heart. This minimally invasive approach is also culturally sensitive because some indigenous communities believe that any manipulation of the heart tarnishes the human soul. So, by offering an alternative to open-heart surgery, the weavers are also respecting the beliefs of parents who would not otherwise allow their children to be operated on, thereby making the treatment more accessible and saving the lives of thousands of children.

I saw another investment in a "risky new idea" that was developed where I live in Seattle, where doctors at the University of Washington Hospital were struggling with pain management in the burn unit. Pain is notoriously difficult to assess, and doctors must constantly walk the line between too little medication and too much. Patients can build up a tolerance to pain medication like opioids, making them less effective, and because they can be so addictive, doctors are often reluctant to prescribe them for fear of abuse. All of this can leave patients in agonizing pain.

Hearing about this challenge, a new solution was proposed by video game creators who created a virtual reality game for patients in the burn unit called Snow World. The game provides an immersive experience that focuses the patient's attention away from the sensation in their bodies (burning) toward the opposite sensation (cold), as they virtually tromp through snowy mountains and throw snowballs at yetis, penguins, and wooly mammoths. Some patients were so distracted by the game that they missed the treatment entirely, asking when the procedure would begin.

I love these examples, because they illustrate so beautifully how great ideas can come from unexpected places, if we have the courage and trust to support them and help them to get the funding they need. As fundraisers, we can become frustrated, exhausted, and burned out when we feel like we are repeating the same patterns over and over again. We get bored. We get irritated. We get nihilistic. We stop getting excited about new and creative ideas.

Imagine instead how excited you would feel to present a new and innovative idea to a funder if you knew they would love it and couldn't wait to be a part of it? Think about all the possibility that comes with innovating. Think about how examples like these might offer new ways to attract new donors, or help current donors make a leap to a much bigger gift to invest in a new and maybe "risky" idea or project?

To raise the funds needed to make your organization sustainable requires a shift away from the traditional fundraising approaches that can keep us trapped in scarcity. Take an abundance mindset, let go of the fear that the idea is too risky, and instead see your role as a way to offer a gift – the opportunity to partner in an exciting new idea and change the world together.

The actions of a single person can have an enormous impact. You, changemaker, can be that connector, that opportunity-creator, that extends a hand to a funder to do life-changing work together. Lean into the risk together.

REFLECTION QUESTIONS

1. Have you ever held back when talking with a funder because you were afraid the ideas might be too risky? What would you do differently in the future?
2. Can you see places where a new and unusual idea or partner could innovate your work?
3. When you think of opportunities to share a new program idea with funders, how does it make you feel? Excitement or fear?

AFFIRMATIONS

- Without risk, there is no reward.
- I trust myself, so that I may model trust.
- Leap and the net will appear.
- I learn the way, on the way.

10

CONNECT TO A VISION OF WHAT'S POSSIBLE: THE GREAT WEALTH TRANSFER TO WOMEN

"I raise up my voice – not so that I can shout, but so that those without a voice can be heard. We cannot all succeed when half of us are held back.

— MALALA YOUSAFZAI

If you've been feeling burned out, changemakers, here's something else that might lift your spirits, in addition to the movements for trusting and centering the needs of nonprofits before donors. The best practices in philanthropy, created by the people who have held the wealth and power, are starting to shift. Over the next decade, an unprecedented amount of assets – over $30 trillion – will shift into the hands of women in the U.S. In fact, it has already started to happen.

If you were not aware of this massive shift, you can be sure the finance sector is indeed watching this carefully, because their future depends on it. Their customer base is going to be changing, and to succeed in their businesses, financial institutions will need to understand women's needs, preferences, and behaviors when it comes to how they want to use their money. And this is significant because until now, wealth management has been a male-dominated field. Not only are the vast majority of financial advisors men (85 percent), and not only are the vast majority of mutual fund managers also men (90 percent), but their customers are also more likely to be men. Less than 1.4 percent of assets under management in the U.S. are managed by diverse teams, and women, particularly women of color, are still sorely underrepresented in financial services. In practical terms, what this means is that when a woman wants to talk to a financial advisor about where she invests her money and which nonprofits she donates to, she most likely won't be talking with another woman. So she likely won't be advised to invest with a gender lens and consider which of the companies she's being advised to invest in have zero women on their board of directors, or which nonprofits have had white men in leadership for the last several decades. You might be thinking, *yes, yes, we all know sexism and racism exist, but why is this significant for nonprofits?*

Today, men are the key financial decision makers in affluent households. But all that is about to change. Your entire board of directors and donors could look completely different a decade from now. Get ready, changemakers.

THE GREAT WEALTH TRANSFER

You may have heard people refer to this major happening as the "Great Wealth Transfer." Most of the conversation has largely been focused on the generational shift of wealth from baby boomers to Gen X, but there are also important gender dynamics to this wealth transfer.

What is the reason for this wealth shifting hands to women? I wish I could say that the answer was that the gender wage gap was finally going away! But alas, we have a long way to go there....Instead, the answer is that women typically live longer than men, so for many women in a heterosexual marriage, this means they will likely inherit *twice* – once from their parents, and then again from their husbands. Further, the data show that when a husband dies and his widow begins making the financial decisions for the household, most women (about 70 percent) will break up with their husband's financial advisor and institution within the first year.

This says a lot about how women view their finances differently, and the importance of finding a financial advisor and institution that will listen to their values. Research shows that many women see the management of their financial assets not merely as trading stocks or investing in Bitcoin to make a profit, but as something that is also values-aligned so that achieving financial goals and making an impact are not mutually exclusive.

Today, roughly 70 percent of assets held by affluent households in the U.S. are controlled by baby boomers. The majority of those assets – about two-thirds – are held in households with heterosexual marriages. As men die, the assets will pass to their spouses, who tend to be both younger and longer lived. In the U.S., women outlive men by an average of five years, and heterosexual women tend to marry partners a couple of years older. By 2030, American women are expected to control much of the $30 trillion in financial assets that baby boomers will possess. The reason this deserves its own chapter is because a wealth transfer of such magnitude approaches the annual GDP of the U.S.

WE ARE THE WORLD

Why is this wealth transfer important to fundraisers? In the words of the famous Lionel Richie song, "We are the world, we are the future." Over the next decade, women will increasingly be the ones to make the financial decisions for their households, and many leading companies are already working to articulate their commitment to meeting women's needs and launching new products (remember the pink Bic pen for women?) that prominently feature women setting up retirement plans and buying houses. Simply by retaining baby-boomer women, financial firms that help women hold their wealth could see one-third higher revenue potential, and adding Gen X and millennial women as clients could provide up to four times more revenue.

This is significant for nonprofit organizations because wealth advisory firms often provide a variety of wrap-around services including philanthropic advising, and this could have a significant impact on their client's charitable giving – which organizations they donate to, how much they invest, and how they structure their giving. The firms that are ready for this could have a significant impact on philanthropy.

This is also significant because if businesses are preparing to have more women as customers, what might this mean for nonprofit donors, board members, and volunteers? It shows just how much capital that may not have been invested in social change before could soon be accessible, simply because women give differently. We can get a glimpse of the future by noticing what is already beginning to happen.

That men have historically held the wealth in this country, and therefore that they would be the ones targeted as donors, is of course very rational. For most of the country's history, since colonization, white men have had a disproportionate share of rights, access and wealth. They were the only ones who could own property, access banks to grow their wealth, and be fairly compensated for their labor. Today, women still hold fewer rights, and even though laws are changing, cultural norms about a woman's place are slow to follow. The Supreme Court's recent decision to overturn Roe v. Wade and restrict the reproductive rights of pregnant people is only one example. Today, the gender wage gap stubbornly persists, the Equal Rights Amendment (ERA) that was introduced in the 1970s has still not been ratified, and a New York Times article highlighted that there are more CEOs named John than women CEOs overall.[1] This explains why the percentage of philanthropy that goes to nonprofits specifically focusing on women and girls still sits stubbornly at less than 2 percent, just as the amount of venture capital that is invested in women-owned businesses is also just over 2 percent.

Wealth is still not equally shared or distributed, making women the largest minority in the world. It is a strange phenomenon to consider women a minority when we are 51 percent of the world, a number that would likely be higher without feticide, and yet, here we are. (I got all my sisters with me.)

However, the very phenomenon of being a minority and then growing wealth is important, because it may explain and shape the way that women give differently.[2] In addition to being more charitable in general, women are more likely to give to causes that support other women, and to give globally, a concept known as social identity theory. That is, beyond supporting nonprofits that affect women and girls in their own communities, such as domestic violence or access to reproductive health, they are also more likely to support organizations in other parts of the world who are addressing the issues holding women and girls back in those communities: access to education for girls, support for climate refugees (80 percent of whom are women and girls), access to menstrual health resources, etc.

In a New York Times article in 2021, "How Women Are Changing the Philanthropic Game," journalist Valeriya Safranova examined how women philanthropists like Melinda Gates, MacKenzie Scott, Priscilla Zuckerberg-Chan, and Lauren Powell Jobs influenced their famous husbands to give more philanthropically.[3] In a Fortune article in 2008, friends of Bill and Melinda Gates credited Melinda for the family's philanthropy, which grew to be the largest foundation in the world.[4] Without her, Mr. Gates said in the profile, "I don't think I'd do as much of it."

And while women giving their time and money is obviously nothing new, for many decades, women gave under their husbands' names, without recognition. Little effort was made to specifically reach out to women as philanthropists, because their volunteer efforts were unrecognized and seen simply as the invisible labor that women should do, and requiring no skill so that, "even a woman can do it." In the article, Debra Mesch, a professor of philanthropy at Indiana University's Lilly Family School of Philanthropy Women's Philanthropy Institute, explained that, "Women who engaged in philanthropy were the behind-the-scenes volunteers, the unrecognized work … the men were the faces."

Again, our best practices in fundraising were built around historic norms, and so for generations, fundraisers have been urged to target white men with the assumption that 1) they hold the wealth, and 2) they make the financial decisions for the household. As a sector, we have missed a crucial opportunity to expand our philanthropic resources simply by not asking women, as well as people of color and people who identify as LGBTQIA+, because of the assumption that they do not hold the resources, and will not be as charitable with their time or money.

This is a lost opportunity, and a best practices myth that needs to change – especially because trillions are about to pass into women's hands. Think of the potential for a sea change! What if women around the country – of all ages, races, and ethnic identities – decided to use their assets in a way that respected people and the planet, and was aligned with their values? We are standing at the precipice of a tremendous opportunity for nonprofits to think differently and make new strides.

For over a century, we have been operating under practices that assume that the money being requested for our nonprofits was created by men, and therefore requests should be made in ways that feel comfortable to men. Imagine what could be possible if we changed the way we do business as usual? Would stuffy meetings in men's only clubs give way to conversations over a walk in the outdoors? Would the insistence on knowing what percentage of funding went to a nonprofit's overhead costs give way to deeper conversations about how the communities being served defined success and what that looked like for them? There are three high-level data points to keep in mind as we dream about what this might look like.

- The first is that women's wealth is rising. Women's share of wealth has risen considerably over the past 50 years and today women hold around 40 percent of global wealth. With this coming wealth transfer, roughly $30 trillion will

shift into women's hands in the U.S. alone over the next decade.
- The second is that the data consistently show that women are more charitable. Across income levels and generations, women are more likely to give, and when they give, they give more than men.
- The third is that women give differently. From motivations, to causes, to behavior, there are gendered differences in giving patterns.

For decades, researchers have asked the question, "Who decides about charitable giving in households?" and numerous studies have been conducted to understand whether and how gender matters in charitable giving. The Women's Philanthropy Institute at the University of Indiana is the leading source of data and has been studying these gendered differences in philanthropy in the greatest detail, because the answers to these questions require looking carefully at the data sets used, methodology employed, and demographic factors included. (For example, one challenge to understanding gendered giving differences is that survey data are often collected at the household level and married couples' giving is combined). Women and men are also obviously not homogeneous groups. By and large, however, the data continue to show, study after study, that women are more charitable, meaning that they are more likely to give, and, on average, they give more than men.

The question of "Who decides?" matters because despite what you may think, most charitable giving in the U.S. comes from individuals and families – not large foundations – whose donations account for 70 percent of all charitable giving. Each household is unique and has different conversations about giving, and this has real-world implications for how much households give, and to what causes and organizations. But it means that many nonprofits should be thinking about their individual giving campaigns as a tremendous source of financial fuel to power their engines.

THE POWER OF THE SHECONOMY

Beyond the high-level data showing that women give more, they also tend to give differently, and their giving seems to produce an amplifier effect. One important way women give differently is by giving in community. That is, rather than making decisions alone or writing an individual check, women often prefer to make decisions about their giving with others. That might take the form of giving circles, through learning series or cohorts with advisors, or by joining women's foundations or local women's funds that offer opportunities to pool their gifts for collective impact.

Giving circles, predominantly comprised of women, have been on the rise over the last decade, and the amount of money they are moving has tripled over the last decade, with an estimated $1.29 billion being granted overall. One beautiful benefit of giving circles is their ability to democratize giving, so that any modest amount has magnified impact when combined with the collective gifts of others in the giving circle. Unlike donor advised funds (DAFs), a tax-free fund where donors can set aside funds to be donated in the future and get an immediate tax benefit regardless of when (or if) they actually donate to a nonprofit, there is little risk that philanthropic assets will remain undistributed, as funding nonprofit organizations is an essential culminating moment for a giving circle.

Further, the donations often go farther because most giving circle donors aren't looking to support major charities, but rather local efforts in their communities that might otherwise be overlooked. Today, the Global Giving Circle Directory created by Grapevine and Philanthropy Together lists more than two thousand giving circles.[5]

A Fidelity Charitable Gift Fund survey also found that women donors were more likely to be public about their gifts than their male counterparts, and had a desire to engage others in charitable activity and to imbue a philanthropic spirit in peers as well as in the next generation of givers. Sharing their experiences with giving may inspire other donors to turn their attention to a previously overlooked cause or organization, thus leveraging the impact of the initial gift. This could be vital for nonprofits, because one gift from such a donor could have a multiplier effect.

Women's funds, too, have shaped how women can give collectively for greater impact. Created by and for women, women's funds – such as a statewide women's foundation that brings women together to fund local organizations together – are generally accompanied by the belief that not only can women's pooled assets contribute more powerfully to social causes when held collectively, but that philanthropic investments in women and girls can accelerate positive change in communities. A report by the Women's Funding Network in 2008 showed that women's funds had distinctive contributions to philanthropy, from their grantmaking impact to their strides in gaining recognition for the importance of investing in women and girls as essential solution-builders.[6] To see evidence that collective giving among women is on the rise, two decades ago the Women's Donor Network had 80 members; today it has 270. A few decades ago, the Women's Funding Network had 20 members; today it has more than 120 and invests $420 million annually in gender equity.

One thing this tells us is that being part of a community – a network such as a Giving Circle, a campaign, or a specific leadership group – is as important as any quantifiable impact from the nonprofit itself. That is, just being asked to be part of a community that is giving together to create change, is equally valuable to the donor. It's not just that the money was invested, but that it was done intentionally, in relationship, and with neighbors, for the good of the community. And as any fundraiser likely knows, the donors closest to you and who already know you are the most likely to increase their gifts.

While the combined giving from a women's fund or a giving circle may seem small in comparison to a large grant from a private foundation, their reach and impact is disproportionately large. This is due to both their focus on investing in women and girls as a catalytic strategy, and their ability to leverage the power of the network in their respective communities. From their earliest days, women's funds have acted as incubators for re-imagining conventional philanthropy, creating new spaces for women to give back to their communities. Many giving circles were incubated by women's funds as a way to create new spaces for women to brainstorm, share, and execute their philanthropic visions.

Giving circles and women's funds help donors to move beyond their roles as charitable benefactors to become active partners working together with nonprofits toward shared goals. Leading women philanthropists have long pointed to the empowerment of women and girls as a successful strategy for achieving shared goals around the world, from climate change to food security to education, health, nutrition, and maternal and infant mortality. By democratizing philanthropy so that anyone, regardless of their wealth, can contribute to a pooled fund, and by using their financial resources to bring opportunity to people in need around the world, women's funds demonstrate a new possibility for how we can resource our most important social causes.

I want to be clear that I am not suggesting that simply changing your donor prospect list to focus on women is a magic bullet that will ensure the financial sustainability of your nonprofit forever and ever. (Wouldn't this make a good Netflix special, though?) I learned that lesson in the nineties when I first entered the field of microcredit, doe-eyed and optimistic that simply helping women access micro-loans would be a panacea to poverty. But what might be possible if you examine the opportunities for new women funders to join you in your organization's work? What might be possible if you take what you know about the ways that women give differently – collectively through pooled funds and giving circles – and consider the opportunities for your own organization or movement?

If you think the transfer of wealth into women's hands is not that significant for the future, consider what our sector might look like with a thousand more MacKenzie Scotts? We can only hope that more women will be inspired by Scott's example and will follow suit, but in the meantime, we can dream of and plan a new future. Imagine how differently your work might look with this new opportunity to find alignment with women funders who are ready to walk with you into the future.

REFLECTION QUESTIONS

1. How might you change your fundraising approaches knowing that your funders will be more likely to be women?
2. Knowing that women give differently, what new opportunities might you create to bring women funders together?
3. Do you see opportunities to center women and girls in your work in a different way?
4. What opportunities for collective giving might boost your fundraising across your donor base?

AFFIRMATIONS

- I offer the opportunity to expand and share abundance from new places.
- New sources of abundance are coming, and I cannot wait to meet them.
- New investments in women will boost our collective efforts toward building a safer, more equitable world.
- I am hopeful and excited for new voices and a more abundant future.

11

HOW TO HAVE FUNDS AND ROSES

"The great force of history comes from the fact that we carry it within us, are unconsciously controlled by it in many ways, and history is literally present in all that we do."

— JAMES BALDWIN

I began this book by talking about the history of how the nonprofit sector was created and how that history shaped toxic practices and myths that still govern our nonprofits today. I hope that, through this book, you are able to see how that can affect the way you see yourself as a fundraiser, your value and worth.

The reason you are feeling burned out is not because you are not good enough, smart enough, or resilient enough. It is because you are working within oppressive systems of patriarchy, white supremacy, and capitalism, all of which are constantly telling you that you are worth less because you work in this sector, that you need to work constantly, that your work must be perfect in order to be accepted, and that your productivity is equal to your worth. None of these things are true. Unfortunately, as we work for social change, we are doing that work inside oppressive systems while we dismantle them. These systems are designed to disconnect us – from ourselves, and from one another. I hope that this book has helped you to become more aware and reflective when that is happening, to practice detoxing those messages from your subconscious, and to reconnect to the circuits that give you energy.

Oppressive systems are designed to keep the status quo, and to make it so exhausting for you to change them and do something different that you eventually fizzle out and give up. Without any action on your part to become aware of when this is happening, brilliant and talented fundraisers like you are likely to burn out.

Let's get a little more technical about how burnout happens, what to do about it, and where our responses such as traditional wellness initiatives fall short so that we can prevent it and heal from it.

To begin, we know that burnout has been on the rise since COVID and is driving employee turnover, and that turnover is highest among funders and founders (usually development directors and executive directors). That means if you are reading this book, you are likely most at risk. Right now, the levels of burnout are at crisis levels for the social change sector. While much has been written about the "Great Resignation" happening since COVID, not as much attention has been paid to how this is affecting the nonprofit sector in particular, which is the safety net supporting many of the people and communities most impacted by COVID.

Even before COVID, the development director role has been known as a "revolving door" position, the hardest to fill and retain by executives, board members, and funders.

Many nonprofit colleagues shake their heads and despair that it is so difficult to find good talent for this role. A colleague who works at a search firm for nonprofits took a deep sigh when I mentioned the words Development Director, saying this is always the most challenging role to fill. The average Development Director role stays vacant for approximately six months before being filled, and, after being hired, they typically do not stay more than two years. Once again, the organization, and perhaps the search firm, too, has to start again.

Consider the effect on our nonprofit organizations, on the sector, and on the movements we are building. A large national nonprofit association found that a whopping 91 percent of their member organizations reported turnover of fundraising staff as one of the biggest problems they face. And turnover is actually much costlier than most people recognize. A study by the *Center for American Progress* found that the costs associated with the turnover of an employee can easily amount to 100 percent of their salary cost. When you factor in additional costs such as lost productivity and the time and expenses associated with hiring and onboarding a replacement, the real cost can approach two to three times the salary for the position. In addition to these direct and indirect costs of finding a replacement, the loss of *relationship capital* – which is central to donor stewardship and fundraising success – can cut fundraising efforts off at the knees.

What is leading to this turnover? The three most widely cited reasons are (1) money – feeling undervalued for the multiple roles development directors are expected to play, (2) culture – unrealistic expectations or lack of support from the board and staff, and (3) burnout – often a result of the first two reasons.

A survey of more than 2,000 nonprofit employees by

Opportunity Knocks found that *half of those surveyed reported feeling burned out in their jobs.* The data has consistently shown that employees who feel burned out are more likely to quit and leave their positions prematurely.

WHY IS BURNOUT SO PREVALENT AMONG FUNDRAISERS?

Dr. Maslach, the researcher who coined the term in 1982, describes burnout as "an erosion of the human soul." The World Health Organization (WHO) now includes burnout in its International Classification of Diseases (ICD-10), describing it as, "a syndrome conceptualized as resulting from chronic workplace stress that has not been successfully managed." Burnout is characterized by three dimensions: (1) feelings of energy depletion or exhaustion, (2) increased mental distance from one's job, or feelings of negativity related to one's job, and (3) feelings of a lack of accomplishment. All of these are the concepts we have been discussing throughout the book.

The WHO definition is important to include here, because it acknowledges that burnout is more than just an employee problem; it's a systemic problem within the sector, and that means that it requires a sectoral solution. Self-care has been the prevention strategy du jour for decades, and yet burnout is on the rise. Why? Because we're ignoring the systemic and institutional factors that are the real causes of burnout.

To address the burnout problem, the first step is to stop blaming individual fundraisers and start looking at the culture of the sector that people are operating within. We should never suggest that if fundraisers had just "manned up" to the workload, or joined a yoga class or "leaned in" that they would have avoided burnout. When it comes to burnout, culture plays a massive role, and this is why burnout has become an epidemic in the nonprofit sector. The expectation is that employees will overwork, and that is reinforced so frequently that it becomes part of the work culture.

While burnout tends to start with exhaustion, we know that what soon follows is shame and self-doubt about our capabilities due to toxic messages all around us. We may begin to feel imposter syndrome and wonder if we are really cut out for this job, and whether all our previous successes were just coincidences. We begin to wonder if the brilliant funding partnership we created in the past can ever truly be replicated or if it was a one-time unicorn. We begin to feel alone, unsupported, and cynical that things can change.

Often times, we go beyond the point of exhaustion and head into the dangerous waters of burnout because we work in a sector that is built around about caring for others. For many of us, socially conditioned as women to be caregivers, we believe that is our role: to be selfless, to literally have *no self*. We tell ourselves, *"You don't need help, there are others that are worse off,"* and to, *"Suck it up."* We function in survival mode, using whatever coping mechanisms and numbing behaviors we can: drinking, over-eating, over-exercising, binging reality tv shows on Netflix (*See? My life isn't so bad, these housewives are a mess!*), and so on. Numbing behaviors also include "revenge bedtime procrastination," when you put off sleeping even when you're tired and you know you should go to bed, because you feel like you didn't have much control over your day. If you feel like you don't have control, then you need to get it from somewhere, and that somewhere is usually right before bed. Numbing behaviors help us to escape reality, or zone out, to avoid the pain of working in a job where we feel undervalued, underpaid, underappreciated, and where there is never an end in sight to the workload or the issues we are addressing. Experiencing imposter syndrome and perfectionism together is one of the strongest predictors of burnout, and this is also why it is so prevalent among women.

Among the biggest reasons for burnout among development professionals, according to the *UnderDeveloped* report by CompassPoint and the Evelyn and Walter J. Haas Fund, are unrealistic expectations, lack of investment in fundraising systems, an unengaged board or leadership, and a poor culture of philanthropy. Taken together, burnout is a complex constellation of toxic practices in the workplace, antiquated best practices, and issues of inequity that have been left unaddressed for far too long.

WHERE OUR RESPONSES TO BURNOUT FALL SHORT

The good news is that burnout is recognizable, preventable, treatable, and reversible. The bad news is that this is not a quick process. This is why, when I work with new nonprofit leaders who are already showing the telltale signs that they are on the fast train to burnout-town, I want to help them to start making changes immediately. You can begin to recover from some of the precursors to burnout within a matter of months. To recover from a toxic workplace that isn't particularly supportive of changing its toxic best practices, however, can take one to two years, according to Dr. Jessica Metcalfe. Once you have hit burnout, it can take *two to five years to recover.* (It definitely took me a few years.) Obviously, this means that it is much easier to prevent burnout before it happens than spend up to five years healing and recovering.

One way that traditional responses to burnout fall short is that they tend to blame the employee. It doesn't do our organizations or our sector any good to take that approach and place the blame for becoming burned out, or the onus of recovering from burnout, on fundraisers alone. All this will do is repeat the cycle and leave a trail of burned out fundraisers behind. Instead, we would be much better served by building strategies into our organizations and our sector that address how our behaviors have led to this phenomenon where half the sector feels burned out.

Another way that traditional responses to burnout fall short is by telling employees to simply address the problem by taking some time for self-care. This approach is like giving an employee a child's tricycle and asking them to keep up with the peleton. As organizations, and as a sector, we need to examine the toxic practices in our organizations that lead to burnout, and we need to take steps toward being accountable for changing those toxic messages and practices. We will not solve this sector-wide challenge by telling employees to "lean in."

Donors, too, have a very important part to play here in examining their role in fundraising burnout and the ways in which they uphold harmful practices and power dynamics. Solutions that only speak to individuals and organizations, but ignore the funders who often hold all the power, will not address the root issues that lead to fundraiser burnout.

FUNDRAISING RESET: 7 STEPS TO TRANSFORM TOXIC PRACTICES THAT LEAD TO BURNOUT

The process of pushing the reset button begins with an awareness that burnout does not happen in a vacuum. It happens gradually, through a series of interactions that leave you feeling small; that your workload is never-ending and is unacknowledged or unrewarded; that your relationships with donors and your team are strained or unfair; and constant messages that you should not complain or rock the boat and instead be a good girl and follow the rules. We heal from these toxic practices by remembering that we are not in this alone, no matter how isolated we feel, and that we are in relationship with one another.

Connecting to Our History

The first step to heal is to connect to our history, to understand how it is that we arrived here. It is important to remember who made the rules that govern our nonprofits today, in what context they were created, and why they feel so painfully antiquated today. As the adage says, to understand where we are going, we must understand where we have been. It is an active and continuous process that requires us to connect the choices of the past to those we face today. To build a more just and equitable future, we must understand our history, because the injustices of the past have informed our attitudes, beliefs, and norms that we experience today. As James Baldwin said, "The great force of history comes from the fact that we carry it within us, are unconsciously controlled by it in many ways, and history is literally present in all we do."

Without knowing how history lives inside us like the parasitic alien in the Sigourney Weaver classic *Alien* (brilliantly described as a sci-fi movie about a scientist with a cat that nobody believes, and therefore everyone dies except her and her cat), we are destined to live our lives and approach our work unconsciously repeating history again and again. It is vital for us to move from the unconscious to conscious action. We must remember that we may not have originally created these rules or these best practices, but we do have agency in dismantling them and replacing them with more just and equitable beliefs. Once we understand where these old ideas and beliefs originated, we have the foundation to understand that they are not serving us (and they never were), that they are, in fact, getting in the way of our work, and that it is time to consciously let them go.

Connect to Yourself

The second step to healing is to connect to ourselves with the full honesty and compassion that we could give to a friend or loved one. What do I mean by this? We often treat ourselves and speak to ourselves very differently than we would to another person that we care about. Our inner critics are fueled by the messages we receive daily in our workplaces, messages that are rooted in historically inequitable beliefs about anyone who is not white, straight, male, able-bodied, cis, etc.... If we witnessed someone that we cared about constantly overworking, feeling unappreciated and misaligned with their work, feeling small and undervalued, and telling themselves that they just needed to play by the rules and suck it up, we would tell them to get the hell out of Dodge. Why, then, do we not use these same voices when we talk to ourselves?

Instead of the compassionate advice we give to others, the most common experiences among the high-achieving changemakers I work with are imposter syndrome, perfectionism, and the go-go-go collision-path toward burnout. We often ignore our somatic mind-body connection. Your mind speaks to your body, and your body speaks to your mind in a constant feedback loop. There is a massive difference in how you choose to show up if you think you are going to fail versus if you think you are going to succeed. If you tell yourself you can't do something, that response will feed the information to your mind, confirming you can't do something. In order to get out of the loop, you must change your words from inner critic to inner badass. When we believe our worth lies in our productivity and we must embrace hustle culture and constantly go-go-go, achieve-achieve-achieve in order to be accepted and loved, we are on a fast-track to exhaustion and burnout. We glorify being busy when we talk with our friends (*I wish I could come to your event, but I am sooo busy*) and we feel guilt and shame for resting. Often, the only reason we stop this constant motion is because our bodies become sick and force us to stop.

Rest and its different forms are important, but the precursor of rest is to reconnect with ourselves, check in with our mind, body, and spirit. If we are feeling defeated and worn down, rather than inspired about our work, we need to be honest with ourselves about that instead of putting on a mask. We need to be compassionate with ourselves when we are not ok instead of muscling through it. If we don't connect with ourselves and listen to what we truly need, that means we have given the choice to someone else. In the words of Mary Oliver, "What will you choose to do with your one, precious life?"

Connect to Your Purpose

Connecting our minds, bodies, and beliefs is vital to shifting how exhausting or unsatisfying our work is, or how meaningful, energizing, and fulfilling our work is. Based on your mindset, you strive for different goals that are personally meaningful based on your worldview. The actions we take are dictated by our perspective of our goals and our purpose. If we are not connected to our sense of purpose, we can achieve a major goal and then feel stuck or unfulfilled afterward. Our beliefs about our purpose are an essential component to unlocking our potential. Your purpose is what motivates you to get out of bed every morning, and connects you to the people and communities you want to fight for. It is how you manifest your beliefs into actions that contribute to making the world a better place.

Knowing that your actions are aligned with your purpose will give you energy, rather than drain it. Even if you have a bad day at work – if a donor treats you with disrespect or your boss is not satisfied with your fundraising efforts – you will know deep in your soul that you are working toward something bigger, and that the metrics of this one particular job do not matter in the greater scheme of things as much as the small but steady steps you take to help push the world toward a safer, more equitable world.

If you are disconnected from, or don't have a clear sense of your purpose, there are some questions you can ask yourself. What gives me the most meaning? What are my greatest pleasures and joy? What is the source of my greatest anxiety? What am I most pleased with? What am I putting my time and energy into? Then, begin paying attention to where you are spending your time and energy. This kind of self-inquiry can usually provide a good indication of where your time and energy are being spent, and whether they are out of alignment with your purpose. Tracking your time and energy can be beneficial, because if you are not spending time on the things that align with your sense of purpose, you will be losing energy, rather than gaining energy, and that can lead you to burnout.

The immediate, short-term goals that occupy your energy, time, and thoughts are probably very specific: to meet next year's operating budget, to create an endowment fund, to build x number of new donor partnerships, etc. But the short-term goal is often subservient to a bigger, more ambitious long-term goal – to supported unhoused people in the community, to provide access to reproductive justice, to improve public policies concerning immigration, etc. Being aware of the purpose you serve to the greater movement, beyond your organization, is important to connect with your purpose. So, too, is connecting with your sacred role in the social change ecosystem.

Connect to Your Community

Deepa Iyer's beautiful visual of the ten archetypes of the social change ecosystem –*Storytellers, Guides, Weavers, Experimenters, Frontline Responders, Visionaries, Caregivers, Builders, Disrupters, and Healers* – can help us locate ourselves within a bigger social justice movement. This visual provides a beautiful link between the universal quest for meaning that drives many funders, and the opportunity to join hands with a nonprofit and activate that desire through a meaningful partnership.

One thing that white supremacy culture does inside our nonprofit and philanthropic sector is to keep us isolated, and to create us and them categories. We distance ourselves from those we serve, calling them beneficiaries, and we distance ourselves from funders, placing them on a pedestal because they have more wealth, and accept whatever they choose to give us, without question. This is a large part of what has led to the critique of the white savior complex, in which predominantly white groups come to communities that are predominantly Black, Indigenous, and people of color (BIPOC) to tell them how best to "develop," implying that there is a right way and that way must emulate those white communities of the global north. It is also what has led to the critique of the nonprofit industrial complex, in which nonprofits feel a greater sense of accountability to their funders, rather than to the communities they serve. The antidote, of course, to this is to reconnect with community.

We cannot heal in isolation. We cannot create social change in isolation. We cannot address burnout in isolation. We need to do this in relationship with community in the same way that we need to reach out to friends for their perspective or for some tough love. Our nonprofit organizations, too, have to play an intentional role in this reset. While every organizational culture is different and there is no one-size-fits-all solution, there are guidelines and approaches we can follow. An organization might adjust its policies to allow employees to decide which holidays are meaningful and which should be abandoned. (For example, do your values align with supporting Columbus Day or with celebrating Juneteenth?) Or, it might choose to provide a meaningful budget for staff to have the professional development support they need (I spent the majority of my nonprofit career literally begging for any professional development support, and was often asked to write proposals to my bosses that took as much time as grant proposals, justifying the costs and expected return on investment for said professional development). Or, it might consider a shorter work week to allow more time for self-care, or unlimited menstrual leave, etc.

Above all else, organizations that want to curb burnout need to create psychological safety for employees to speak candidly without fear of losing their jobs, including speaking freely about the silos that distance nonprofit fundraisers, funders, and the communities they serve.

Connect to What Nourishes You

We go through life thinking we are rested because we have gotten enough sleep the night before, but in reality, we are still exhausted. The result is a culture of high-achievers, usually women, that can easily become burned out. We suffer from a "rest deficit" because we don't understand the true power of rest, which is restoration. We must remember that rest is vital, not a luxury, and that without it, we will not be able to do our world-changing work.

Connect to Trust

This is where reconnecting to an abundance mindset, rather than a scarcity mindset, is a powerful antidote. We design our programs, determine how much staff will be paid, and create strategic plans based on what we believe is possible, and often our visions are clouded by scarcity and worst-case scenarios in which there is not enough money, donors, board members, influence, or time. Surrounded by that belief system day in and day out, we begin to believe that this is true and that there are not enough resources for what you ultimately want to accomplish in your organization.

Scarcity is a profound psychological impediment, because if your assumption is one of constant lack, this becomes your reality, and it shows up in the way you approach conversations with funders, assuming they won't want to partner with you or invest in your vision. In truth, there is an abundance of donors, supporters, influential advocates, board members, collaborators, partners, and funding. Don't believe me? Today, there is over $234 billion (yes, you read that right) sitting in donor-advised funds, waiting to be invested in nonprofit organizations like yours.

There are also countless new ideas, new leaders, and powerfully life-changing partnerships that could radically accelerate our progress on some of these issues, but we have not yet invested in them because they seem too risky. While much of the onus of investing in "risky" people and ideas is on funders, nonprofit leaders like yourself also play a role in this. As frontline connectors with funders, you can advocate for these new ideas. You can encourage funders to take risks and bets on new partners. This abundance is waiting for you to tap into it. If you start by simply believing that there is enough, even though you cannot see it yet and have no idea where it is, the sky is the limit.

Connect to a Vision of What's Possible

At the beginning of this book, I shared with you an experience where a board member told me that my idea to shift the focus of our organization's work on land rights to a gendered spotlight on the importance of women's land rights was a risky idea that could damage our credibility, because then we would be seen as "a women's rights organization." If I had chosen to listen to that "no" from one of our biggest donors and power-holders as chair of our board of directors, the world would look very different. I held a vision of what could be possible, even when it seemed like everyone would say no, and even when my boss told me to drop it. It seemed crazy, risky, and even dangerous. But so, too, is continuing to do the same things and expect different results.

We know that what is currently happening in our nonprofit organizations and in our sector is making us sick, disillusioned, and burnt out. We know that women, people of color, people who are LGBTQIA+, and people with disabilities are still often missing from our nonprofits because these toxic practices drive them away, and thereby deprive all of us of their wisdom and brilliance. So what are we truly risking by taking the time to shift our minds, nourish our bodies, and dream of a different future? In truth, we have nothing to lose and everything to gain.

My wish for you, changemaker, is to be able to recognize the toxic practices that we have been taught are the gold standard in the industry, and to detox and transform them to free yourself and reconnect with your purpose.

My dream for you, changemakers, is that you can use this book to reflect on how you approach your work and your purpose because the world needs you. We are the ones we have been waiting for. We are each other's harvests.

I hope that you can recommit to your values and to understanding the history of where we have been so that you understand what to let go of that is not serving you. I hope that you feel strong enough in your values that you could comfortably turn down Melinda Gates if she was not aligned. And I hope that you are inspired and excited as I am for women to finally be meaningfully included in the financial sector and to revolutionize philanthropy, just as microcredit revolutionized the finance sector by turning what was invisible into the visible and the powerful.

Beyond all else, I hope that you feel valued, appreciated, honored, and revered for the important work you do. As Ram Dass says, "We are all just walking each other home."

ACKNOWLEDGMENTS

For my wife, who supported my dream to write this book and watered my garden for me when I needed more time to finish each chapter.

For my friends, who held my vision and sent me funny cat memes when I was feeling overwhelmed.

For my family, who always reminds me that my origin story was that I was grown from a bean sprout.

For every colleague who has ever cried in my office, and for everyone who let me cry in theirs.

For Angela, Cory, and Natasa at Difference Press who walked me through the surreal process of writing a book.

For all the animals that appeared as I wrote this book, including my dog Xola, the runaway parakeet El Chapo that showed up on our doorstep one day, and the crows staring at me outside my office right now.

GLOSSARY OF TERMS

- Executive Director / CEO: The titles executive director and chief operating officer (CEO) are both used throughout the nonprofit sector. For the purposes of this book, I use executive director or ED to mean both.
- Development Director: In the nonprofit sector, there are various titles used for the highest-ranking fund-development staff position: Director of Advancement, Director of Philanthropy, Director of Development, etc. For the purposes of this book, I use the title development director to mean the staff person in the highest ranking development position within the organization.
- Development: Development is the process of cultivating relationships with people who will support a nonprofit organization. Cultivation is defined as any activity that builds awareness and connection for donors / funders and prospective donors / funders with your organization, and

increases your understanding of why someone might give to your organization. Fund development includes fundraising which is the specific methods used to secure charitable donations (e.g. annual fund, face-to-face asks, online, proposals, etc.).

- Culture of philanthropy: While familiar to fundraising professionals, the term "culture of philanthropy" is not commonly used outside the sector. Not to be confused with grantmaking or the act of giving money as a donor, a "culture of philanthropy" refers to a set of organizational values and practices that support development within a nonprofit organization. For the purposes of this book, I use the following definition: Most people in the organization act as ambassadors and engage in relationship building. Everyone promotes philanthropy and can articulate a case for giving. Fund development is viewed and valued as a mission-aligned program of the organization. Organizational systems are established to support donors. The executive director is committed and personally involved in fundraising.
- Funding Ecosystem: A funding ecosystem reveals a web of connectivity between movements and funders, and makes a fundamental distinction between direct funding – money that reaches movements – and money that could reach movements, but does not.
- Intersectional Funding: "Grant-making that takes into consideration the ways in which multiple systems of oppression are interwoven

in people's lives, communities, cultures, and institutions and how they impact people differently based on where each person sits and their lived experience." (Definition from *Journey Towards Intersectional Grantmaking* (2018), Funders for a Just Economy, https://www.nfg.org/resources/journey-towards-intersectional-grant-making)
- Transformational Funding Framework: A conceptual foundation that acknowledges the systemic oppressions that perpetuate inequality. Instead of viewing people only as beneficiaries of particular services or programs, transformational funding frameworks recognize their political agency and voice, flowing resources directly to communities to challenge and transform power relations and structures.
- Transformational Funding Practices: Some examples of transformational funding practices include:

1. Prioritizing core support and / or unrestricted funding
2. Trusting grantees, local leaders, and communities as experts of their own lived realities
3. Finding ways to decentralize power and decisions to ensure grantees are connected to decision-making processes
4. Communicating with transparency about funding limitations and requirements
5. Partnering with other funders to overcome limitations or barriers

ABOUT THE AUTHOR

Radha Friedman is a philanthropic advisor with over two decades of experience in funding social justice efforts around the world. As the founder of her own philanthropic consulting and coaching practice, she has overseen over 100 grants on five continents and is on a mission to mobilize more investments in women and historically underfunded communities. She is host of the *Radhacal Good* podcast, which was ranked by Spotify in the top 20 percent most shared podcasts globally.

Radha has been a consultant and advisor to the Bill & Melinda Gates Foundation on their gender equality strategy, the Clinton Global Initiative's Network on Women & Girls Economic Empowerment, and has worked with individual donors, foundations, and Fortune 500 companies seeking to make their greatest impact by investing in nonprofits. Her work has engaged luminaries including the Dalai Lama, actor Kristen Bell, and (the notorious) Justice Ruth Bader Ginsburg. Radha has also helped nonprofit organizations earn global awards for their work, including the Hilton Humanitarian Prize and the Skoll Award for Social Entrepreneurship.

Radha's work is grounded by an M.A. in International Development Studies and M.S. in Public Service Administration from DePaul University, a B.A. in South Asian Studies from Antioch College, and a post-graduate certificate in Cross-Sector Partnerships from the University of Cambridge. She has been named a fellow by the United Nations Alliance of Civilizations, the American Express Foundation, the Independent Sector, the Henry M. Jackson Foundation, and the Global Women's Leadership Network.

Radha lives in Seattle with her wife, dog, and rescue parakeet.

THANK YOU FOR READING

Thank you so much for reading *Fundraising Without Burnout: Reimagining Philanthropy to Radically Transform Your Impact.*

I love each and every one of you who opened this book and read it from the first chapter to the last. You rock!

Since you've finished reading this book, I know that you are on the path to leaving behind the toxic practices that have been draining you and claiming your role in transforming philanthropy as we enter into the largest wealth transfer in history.

Visit www.fundraisingwithoutburnout.com/readergift for a free masterclass that you can take to reimagine your impact and to rebalance your energy!

I would love to learn more about your journey and your success in your world-changing work. Please keep in touch via LinkedIn, Instagram, and TikTok, share your wins (tag me and use #fundraisingburnout), and visit fundraisingwithoutburnout.com for more resources.

I'm passionate about ensuring that women and girls have the rights and resources they need to thrive, particularly in places in the world where resources are less accessible. Part of the income from this book and my other programs will support locally-led nonprofits that center women and girls or color. Thank you for supporting these women and girls, too.

NOTES

1. THE FUNDRAISER REVOLUTION

1. Flandez, R. 2012. The cost of high turnover in fundraising jobs. *The Chronicle of Philanthropy.* https://www.philanthropy.com/article/The-Cost-of-High-Turnover-in/226573
2. Bell, Jeanne and Marla Cornelius, 2013. *UnderDeveloped: A National Study of Challenges Facing Nonprofit Fundraising.* San Francisco: CompassPoint Nonprofit Services and the Evelyn and Walter Haas, Jr. Fund,
3. Maslach C, and Gomes M (2006) Overcoming burnout. In MacNair R (ed) *Working for Peace: A Handbook of Practical Psychology.* 2nd ed. San Luis Obispo: Impact Publishers.

4. CONNECT TO YOUR HISTORY: HOW FUNDRAISING BECAME GENDERED

1. Carnegie, Andrew, 1835-1919. *The Gospel of Wealth, and Other Timely Essays.* Garden City, New York: Doubleday, Doran & Company, Inc., 1933.
2. Miller, Kevin, and Vagins, Deborah. *Broken Ladders: Barriers to Women's Leadership in Nonprofit Organizations.* The American Association of University Women. May 2018.
3. Moss Lee, Danielle. July, 2020. *Black Women in Nonprofits Matter*, Nonprofit Quarterly.
4. Scott, Roxanne. January 2017. *If Women Rule the Fundraising Game, Why Don't They Hold More Top Positions?*, Louisville Public Media.
5. Kochnar, Rakesh. March 2023. *The Enduring Grip of the Gender Pay Gap.* Pew Research Center.
6. Allison, Paul, England, Paula, and Levanon, Asaf. December 2009. *Occupational Feminization and Pay: Assessing Causal Dynamics Using 1950-2000 U.S. Census Data.* The University of North Carolina Press.

6. CONNECT TO YOUR PURPOSE

1. Iyer, Deepa. *Social Change Now: A Guide for Reflection and Connection.* Available at: https://www.socialchangemap.com
2. Craig, Nick and Snook, Scott A. May 2014. *From Purpose to Impact.* Harvard Business Review.
3. Brown, Adrienne Maree. 2017. *Emergent Strategy.* AK Press

7. CONNECT TO COMMUNITY

1. Carmichael, Allistair, Dillon, Roland, Ferraris, Erin, and King, Jemma. *Supporting resilience and preventing burnout in nonprofits.* April 2023. McKinsey & Co.
2. Gorski, Paul and Erakat, Noura. 2019. *Racism, whiteness, and burnout in antiracism movements: How white racial justice activists elevate burnout in racial justice activists of color in the United States.* Sage Journals.
3. https://www.trustbasedphilanthropy.org/
4. https://communitycentricfundraising.org/
5. https://www.participatorygrantmaking.org

8. CONNECT TO NOURISHMENT

1. Hersey, Tricia. 2022. *Rest Is Resistance: A Manifesto.* New York : Little, Brown Spark
2. *Idem.*
3. Dalton-Smith, Saundra. 2017. *Sacred Rest: Recover Your Life, Renew Your Energy, Restore Your Sanity.*

10. CONNECT TO A VISION OF WHAT'S POSSIBLE: THE GREAT WEALTH TRANSFER TO WOMEN

1. Wolfers, Justin. 2015. *Fewer Women Run Big Companies Than Men Named John.* New York Times.
2. Gender Trends: The causes men and women prefer when donating through GiveNow. Available at: https://www.ourcommunity.com.au/general/general_article.jsp?articleid=7659
3. Safranova Valeriya. June 2021. *How Women Are Changing the Philanthropy Game*, New York Times.
4. Sellers, Patricia. 2008. *Melinda Gates Goes Public.* Fortune

5. The Global Giving Circle Directory is available at: https://www.grapevine.org/grapevine-giving-circle-directory
6. *Accelerating Change for Women and Girls: The Role of Women's Funds.* By the Women's Funding Network and The Foundation Center, 2008.